Effective Communications for Project Management

OTHER AUERBACH PUBLICATIONS

Agent-Based Manufacturing and Control Systems: New Agile Manufacturing Solutions for Achieving Peak Performance
Massimo Paolucci and Roberto Sacile
ISBN: 1574443364

Curing the Patch Management Headache
Felicia M. Nicastro
ISBN: 0849328543

Cyber Crime Investigator's Field Guide, Second Edition
Bruce Middleton
ISBN: 0849327687

Disassembly Modeling for Assembly, Maintenance, Reuse and Recycling
A. J. D. Lambert and Surendra M. Gupta
ISBN: 1574443348

The Ethical Hack: A Framework for Business Value Penetration Testing
James S. Tiller
ISBN: 084931609X

Fundamentals of DSL Technology
Philip Golden, Herve Dedieu,
and Krista Jacobsen
ISBN: 0849319137

The HIPAA Program Reference Handbook
Ross Leo
ISBN: 0849322111

Implementing the IT Balanced Scorecard: Aligning IT with Corporate Strategy
Jessica Keyes
ISBN: 0849326214

Information Security Fundamentals
Thomas R. Peltier, Justin Peltier,
and John A. Blackley
ISBN: 0849319579

Information Security Management Handbook, Fifth Edition, Volume 2
Harold F. Tipton and Micki Krause
ISBN: 0849332109

Introduction to Management of Reverse Logistics and Closed Loop Supply Chain Processes
Donald F. Blumberg
ISBN: 1574443607

Maximizing ROI on Software Development
Vijay Sikka
ISBN: 0849323126

Mobile Computing Handbook
Imad Mahgoub and Mohammad Ilyas
ISBN: 0849319714

MPLS for Metropolitan Area Networks
Nam-Kee Tan
ISBN: 084932212X

Multimedia Security Handbook
Borko Furht and Darko Kirovski
ISBN: 0849327733

Network Design: Management and Technical Perspectives, Second Edition
Teresa C. Piliouras
ISBN: 0849316081

Network Security Technologies, Second Edition
Kwok T. Fung
ISBN: 0849330270

Outsourcing Software Development Offshore: Making It Work
Tandy Gold
ISBN: 0849319439

Quality Management Systems: A Handbook for Product Development Organizations
Vivek Nanda
ISBN: 1574443526

A Practical Guide to Security Assessments
Sudhanshu Kairab
ISBN: 0849317061

The Real-Time Enterprise
Dimitris N. Chorafas
ISBN: 0849327776

Software Testing and Continuous Quality Improvement, Second Edition
William E. Lewis
ISBN: 0849325242

Supply Chain Architecture: A Blueprint for Networking the Flow of Material, Information, and Cash
William T. Walker
ISBN: 1574443577

The Windows Serial Port Programming Handbook
Ying Bai
ISBN: 0849322138

AUERBACH PUBLICATIONS

www.auerbach-publications.com
To Order Call: 1-800-272-7737 • Fax: 1-800-374-3401
E-mail: orders@crcpress.com

Effective Communications for Project Management

Ralph L. Kliem

Auerbach Publications
Taylor & Francis Group
Boca Raton   New York

Auerbach Publications is an imprint of the
Taylor & Francis Group, an **informa** business

Auerbach Publications
Taylor & Francis Group
6000 Broken Sound Parkway NW, Suite 300
Boca Raton, FL 33487-2742

© 2008 by Taylor & Francis Group, LLC
Auerbach is an imprint of Taylor & Francis Group, an Informa business

---

Library of Congress Cataloging-in-Publication Data

Kliem, Ralph L.
    Effective communications for project management / Ralph L. Kliem.
       p. cm.
    Includes bibliographical references and index.
    ISBN-13: 978-1-4200-6246-5 (alk. paper)
    1. Project management. 2. Communication in organizations. I. Title.

HD69.P75K578 2008
658.4'04--dc22
                                      2007015619

Visit the Taylor & Francis Web site at
http://www.taylorandfrancis.com

and the Auerbach Web site at
http://www.auerbach-publications.com

Dedication

Priscilla, Tonia, Mom, Dad, Rambo, and Skipper

Contents

Preface..xi

Figures..xiii

About the Author xv

Chapter 1
The Elements of Project Communications Management................1
Five Basic Communications Truths Facing Project Managers....................3
Understanding the Communications Process 5
The Communications Process...7
Sender and Receiver...8
Message 10
Medium...11
Feedback..13
Variables 15
Setting 17
At the Center 21
A Difficult Process 22
References...22

Chapter 2
Establishing the Project Management Information System.........25
Definition and Components 25
Key Characteristics 27
Roles..28
Developing an Automated PMIS 28
Data Versus Information...30
Types of Repositories 34
Keys to Making a PMIS Meaningful...35
Fine Distinction.. 40
Never-Ending Construction 40

Chapter 3
Personality Style and Communications 45
Caveats 45
The Myers–Briggs Temperament 46
The Birkman Model..49
Color Code 50
Multiple Intelligences 51
Enneagram 53
Herrmann Brain Dominance..56
Organizational Engineering..57
Many Models...59

Chapter 4
Applying Active and Effective Listening 63
Project Management Information System (PMIS) Contributions 63
Active and Effective Listening..63
Two Important Reasons.. 64
Why Few People Listen Effectively 64
Four Steps for Effective and Active Listening........................65
Hear..65
Clarify.. 66
Interpret 67
Respond 67
The Most Important Skill 68

Chapter 5
Preparing the Communications Management Plan and
Establishing an Issues Management Process 71
Contributions of the Project Management Information System (PMIS) 71
Communications Management Plan..72
Characteristics 72
Challenges 73
Making the CMP a Reality..75
CMP Implementation Suggestions 78
Issues Management Process 79
Issues Management Challenges... 80
Significant Contributor... 80

Chapter 6
Drafting and Publishing Documentation 83
Contributions of the Project Management Information System (PMIS) 83
Why Writing Matters 83
Too Little Importance... 84

Project Manager as Writer 85
Documentation Phases 86
 Draft 86
  Defining Readers 88
  Determining Goals 88
  Conducting Research 88
  Preparing an Outline 90
  Creating the Document... 90
 Conducting the Review..95
 Revising the Manuscript 96
 Receiving Approval or Disapproval 96
 Publishing or Distributing the Document......................96
 Maintaining and Updating Documents 97
Different Types of Supporting Material 97
Common Types of Documentation 98
The Project Manual 103
The Right Amount..104

Chapter 7
Conducting Meetings

Conducting Meetings...**109**
PMIS Contributions 109
Reasons for Meetings...109
Reasons for Meeting Failure 110
Indicators of Poor Meetings.. 110
Key Steps for Successful Meetings 111
Planning the Meeting 111
Conducting the Meeting..113
Follow up on Results... 115
Holding Effective Virtual Meetings 115
Passing through the Impasse.. 116
Dealing with "Bad Eggs" 119
Rules for Meetings 121
Worst and Best of Times.. 121

Chapter 8
Giving Effective Presentations

Giving Effective Presentations..**125**
PMIS Contributions 125
Many Opportunities to Present 125
Loss of Effectiveness...126
Types of Presentations...127
Characteristics of an Effective Presentation........................127
Preparation 130

Rehearsal 137
Delivery 140
Post Delivery... 151
Summary 152

Chapter 9
Developing and Deploying a Web Site 167
PMIS Contributions 167
Three Main Advantages 167
Two Main Challenges... 168
Important Guidelines 168
Sharing and Visibility 173

Chapter 10
Building War Rooms 175
PMIS Contributions 175
Many Pluses... 175
Key Steps 176
Challenges 180
Valuable Asset 181

Chapter 11
The Key to Effective Leadership..185
PMIS Requires Good Data... 185
PM Disciplines Not Enough.. 186
Leadership 186

References...189
Books... 189
Articles 192

Glossary..199

Index...209

Preface

Project managers spend at least 80 to 90 percent of their time communicating on projects. Time and again, however, studies by professional organizations and think tanks with an interest in project management have revealed that communications remains one of the top problems confronting projects in general and project managers in particular. Based upon what I have witnessed in my career, these findings are right on. Communications remains one of the major differentiators between project success and failure.

The reality is that projects don't just happen. To succeed, projects require a concentrated effort on the part of two or more people to communicate effectively. It is the job of the project manager to lay the groundwork for ensuring good communication occurs throughout the life cycle of a project. Just as importantly, it is the job of the project manager to make sure that good communication continues to the very end of a project.

In many respects, the quality of all output on a project depends on the effectiveness of communications. When communications deteriorates, a strong likelihood will exist that so does the quality of the deliverables resulting from the efforts of everyone on a project. Bad communications, therefore, often equates to bad results; good communications often equates to good results.

Most project managers might view that statement as common sense; apparently very little of this common sense exists on projects. Few projects finish on time, within budget, and meet requirements. Most miss two of the criteria and much of the time the dismal results are directly related to poor communications with many of the major organizations and individuals having an interest in the outcome of a project – the stakeholders.

It's unfortunate that communications on many projects tend to have the finesse of two heavyweight fighters talking to each other prior to a championship event at Madison Square Gardens. What communications that does occur seems to occur spontaneously and without any coordinated purpose.

In this book, I present the essential elements of effective communications on projects. These elements have worked for me and other project managers with whom I have had the honor to work with over many years. By applying all or even a few of these elements on your projects, you will increase the likelihood of success many times over. By ignoring them, you will increase the likelihood of failure. In the end, it's your choice.

Figures

Figure 1.1   Project managers as linchpins..2
Figure 1.2   Bad communications equals higher costs. 3
Figure 1.3   The communications process..6
Figure 1.4   Circle network. 18
Figure 1.5   Wheel network......................................19
Figure 1.6   Linear network......................................19
Figure 1.7   Y network......................................20
Figure 1.8   Hierarchical network. 20
Figure 1.9   Relational network. 21
Figure 1.10 PMIS and project communications management skills. 21
Figure 2.1   PMIS flowchart......................................29
Figure 2.2   Logical model. 37
Figure 2.3   Physical model. 38
Figure 3.1   Myers–Briggs temperament summary table. 46
Figure 3.2   Myers–Briggs temperament (preferences) summary table. 48
Figure 3.3   Birkman model summary table......................................49
Figure 3.4   Color code summary table. 50
Figure 3.5   Multiple intelligence summary table. 52
Figure 3.6   Enneagram summary table. 53
Figure 3.7   Herrmann brain dominance summary table. 56
Figure 3.8   Organizational engineering summary table. 58
Figure 4.1   Listening flowchart. 65
Figure 5.1   Communications management plan flowchart......................75
Figure 5.2   Issues management flowchart......................................79
Figure 5.3   Critical issues/action item log......................................80
Figure 6.1   Documentation flowchart. 87
Figure 6.2   Example of a well-written memo......................................91
Figure 6.3   Example of a policy. 98
Figure 6.4   Example of project procedure written in step-by-step format. 99
Figure 6.5   Example of project procedure written in playscript format. 100
Figure 6.6   Example of project procedure written in narrative format. 101

Figure 7.1   Meetings flowchart. 111
Figure 7.2   Agenda for a checkpoint (gate) review. 112
Figure 7.3   Agenda for a project staff meeting. 112
Figure 7.4   Agenda for a status review meeting. 113
Figure 7.5   Agenda for a change board meeting. 114
Figure 7.6   Agenda for a daily standup meeting. 114
Figure 7.7   Thinking hats summary table. 117
Figure 7.8   Difficult people summary table. 119
Figure 8.1   Outline of an informative presentation. 128
Figure 8.2   Outline of a persuasive presentation. 129
Figure 8.3   Outline of an explanatory presentation. 129
Figure 8.4   Presentation flowchart. 129
Figure 8.5   Preparation flowchart. 130
Figure 9.1   Web site flowchart. 169
Figure 9.2   Hierarchy chart. 171
Figure 10.1 War room flowchart. 176
Figure 10.2 War room wall number 1. 178
Figure 10.3 War room wall number 2. 179
Figure 10.4 War room wall number 3. 179

About the Author

Ralph L. Kliem has over twenty-five years of experience with Fortune 500 firms in the financial and aerospace industries. His wide, varied experience in project and program management includes managing compliance and information technology projects and programs.

In addition to being the author of over 15 books that have been translated in several languages, he has published more than 200 articles in leading business and information systems publications.

Mr. Kliem is an adjunct faculty member of City University in Seattle and a former one with Seattle Pacific University; an instructor with Bellevue Community College; and a frequent presenter to the Puget Sound chapter of the Project Management Institute and other professional organizations. He also teaches PMP certification and other project management seminars and workshops in the United States and Canada.

He can be reached at Ralph.Kliem@verizon.net

Chapter 1

The Elements of Project Communications Management

Communications on a project is a challenging, ongoing process for a project manager and all stakeholders. Project managers, however, have perhaps the greater challenge because of their position. All communication flows through them and, often, from them (Figure 1.1). They are akin to a communications center that regulates the communications process.

Project managers are about the only ones who communicate regularly with many stakeholders at multiple levels within an organization. They communicate with immediate team members who are the ones who produce the deliverables for the final product. They communicate with functional managers, such as those at the first and second levels of the corporate organization, to obtain resources. They communicate with senior managers and executives regarding project status. They communicate with the customer from technical and general business perspectives to clarify information and receive approvals. They set up the communications infrastructure to support the overall project. It is quite easy to see, therefore, that the ability to communicate is a crucial competence that project managers must possess to expect a successful outcome for their projects.

Unfortunately, this competence on projects is rarer than people might think, as indicated by several studies.

According to a study by *Vital Smarts* magazine, 70 percent of 10,000 projects in Fortune 500 firms failed because people did not communicate that something

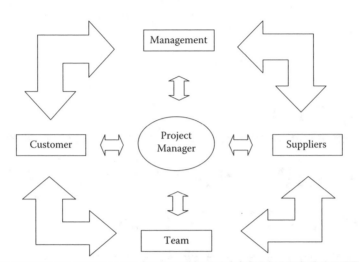

Figure 1.1 Project managers as linchpins.

was wrong, resulting in negative consequences from a cost, schedule, and quality perspective.[1]

Another survey, focused on IT projects, reflected a host of specific problems associated with communications. The top ten concerns centered on communications about requirements: they were ambiguous, too overwhelming to comprehend, and inconsistent.[2]

Still another survey by the Center for Business Practice identified ten key management challenges, which included two problems with communications: limited visibility of activities and no project management information system (PMIS).[3]

BULL conducted a study that found 57 percent of project failures resulted from "bad" communications among stakeholders.[4]

These and many other studies are interesting in that they reflect, to a certain degree, project managers' inability to inculcate effective communications in projects.

Communications problems, of course, are not unique to the project management environment; they are part of much larger organizations.

A study noted in *InformationWeek* showed that 30–40 percent of IT managers complain about communications-related data and information: receiving too much, no one sharing, and trying to decide what is current or has been previously received.[5]

Another study by Prewitt identified several contributors to the IT leadership failure. Most of them relate directly to communications failure: poor interpersonal skills, not acknowledging problems, and weak management skills.[6]

Regardless of the field they are in, it is fair to say that project managers face monumental challenges when instituting good communications on projects and

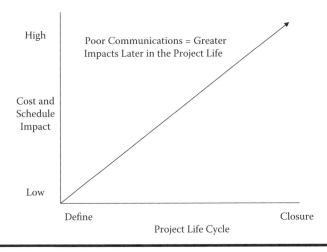

High

Cost and
Schedule
Impact

Low

Poor Communications = Greater
Impacts Later in the Project Life

Define   Closure

Project Life Cycle

Figure 1.2   Bad communications equals higher costs.

wanting to become expert communicators themselves. The challenges become even more acute when dealing with global and geographically dispersed teams using the latest technology, and with stakeholders who must apply very specialized skills. Although all project management skills are critical, project managers must recognize the importance of effective communications on their projects. Indeed, a strong argument can be made that poor communications can result in poor application of skills in other areas.

What's worse, poor communications can have a costly impact on projects as they progress through project life cycles (Figure 1.2). When communications fail in the beginning, such as when assumptions and goals are being defined, the opportunity to correct the situation later becomes more difficult and costly. Projects gain momentum, and few people want to hold them up while ways are found to improve communications. Any effort to rectify poor communications can result in slowing momentum and causing rework. What's worst, the damage may not surface until the product or service is in production, leading to maintenance nightmares.

Five Basic Communications Truths Facing Project Managers

Unfortunately, project managers often misunderstand the complexity behind communications even though they spend most of their time communicating. Here are five self-evident communications truths that impact their performance yet are often overlooked.

Communicating is about people, not media. The reality is that many project managers think that the communications media they employ will solve any communications problem. Nothing can be further from the truth. For example, an e-mail does not produce clarity of communications any better than a pen. So the use of computers does not guarantee cooperation. What is important is the message and tailoring it to the appropriate audience. Unfortunately, many project managers apply media with the finesse of an unsharpened meat cleaver.

The fact is that communications require careful consideration. Communicating effectively requires determining who must receive the message, in what format, and when; it must include feedback to ascertain its effectiveness.

Communications are ongoing throughout the project life cycle. Unfortunately, many project managers seem to forget that fact. Often, they become engaged with technical concerns and overlook their pivotal role as the communications focal point of their projects. Perhaps, they communicate only during the earlier phases of a project and then trust the momentum of these first directions to take over and bring the project home successfully. Or just the reverse happens: they ignore communication during the early phases, thinking that only later will the need arise.

Project managers should realize that communication is ongoing, through all project phases. Communications don't cease until the project finishes, and, in fact, each phase provides its own need for exchanging ideas. Managers must keep everyone in touch and adapt their approach to meet the ever-changing needs of their projects.

Communications are affected by the context of the environment. Because the environment is in flux and the project represents change in itself, challenges to communications are ever present. These changes will impact a project manager's approach toward communicating. For example, under some circumstances, certain face-to-face meetings make more sense than virtual sessions; under other circumstances, it might be the opposite.

Many project managers, however, fail to consider the context of their environment. They frequently apply the same media or techniques to communicate. Often, the rationale is that if it worked on one project, then it should on another. One size fits all, from their perspective; the result is using a medium or technique in a way that is akin to putting a square peg in a round hole.

Communications occur in various forms and at different levels. This point is somewhat tied to the previous one. Not all media and techniques of communication are the same. Each one has its unique application and is geared to a specific audience. Stakeholders at the executive level, for example, have communications preferences and needs that are different from those of the core team. In the contemporary environment where an overabundance of data and information exists, the earmarking of communications media and techniques becomes even more important. Horizontal and vertical communications must be adapted to the needs of whoever is receiving the data and information.

The challenge for project managers is to adapt and be flexible when communicating. They must learn how to communicate to a wide variety of audiences to varying degrees of abstraction and specificity. They must choose the appropriate medium and tailor the messages to a particular audience. In other words, mass communications no longer work.

Communications is about information rather than data. Data, in itself, is meaningless. In fact, if more data is provided, the likelihood is that its value will start to decrease arithmetically and maybe even geometrically. The amount of data can become so voluminous that it becomes incomprehensible, drowning its victim. The result is not a paperless office but one with mountains of paper filling cubicles and offices. The separation of significant and insignificant data becomes indistinguishable.

Many project managers, often unwittingly, contribute to this flood of data. They think churning more data is better, serving as an indicator of productivity and progress. Unfortunately, it does just the opposite, obscuring anything significant. The key is to provide information, that is, data with meaning, in a format and level of abstraction geared to the right people. Information is processed data that serves some purpose, such as an indicator of a variance to the budget or schedule target of work packages. To provide information, project managers need to develop an effective communications plan that serves not only their own needs but also those of stakeholders. Essentially, project managers must function as intelligence professionals, separating significant information from the mass of insignificant detail.

Understanding the Communications Process

To communicate effectively, project managers must have a good understanding of the communications process (Figure 1.3). However, before describing the process, it is first important to understand some of its characteristics.

Communications is an integrated and interdependent process between two or more people. To communicate effectively, two or more people must be involved, one to send something and the other to receive it. These roles can change dramatically during the course of communications. The sender can become the recipient, and the recipient can become the sender. When communications occurs in this manner, a free flow of data and, more importantly, of information can happen. When the roles do not shift—that is, when the sender and receiver do not exchange roles— the communications process begins to deteriorate; the exchange of information declines and it becomes more of a process for distributing data rather than information. An exchange between the sender and receiver must occur if the process is to prove effective. Integration and interdependence are two essential characteristics for an effective communications process to occur. However, integration and interdependence are not enough.

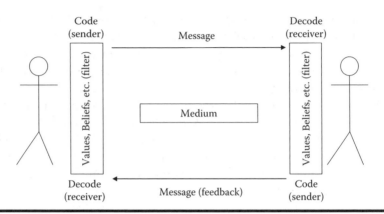

Figure 1.3   The communications process.

Communications is a complex, dynamic process. It never remains static, meaning that the sender sends the message and the recipient responds. Instead, the exchange between two or more individuals takes place over a period of time and a number of factors can affect how these people send and respond. At one moment, the approach and information may prove effective, and, at another, quite difficult. Many influencing factors and barriers can arise at one point in time and then may not even exist at another. Hence, a medium or strategy can work at one moment and totally fail at another. Internal (e.g., psychological) and external factors (e.g., organizational changes) can both add to this complex, dynamic process.

Communications is an ongoing, never-ending process. It never occurs just once but continues throughout the life cycle of a project. For project managers it remains an important function through the completion of the last task; even then, it may continue. To add to the challenge, project managers must adapt their communications to the unique requirements of each project phase and those of the different stakeholders.

Many project managers focus on one or two phases of the life cycle, usually those that interest them the most. The problem is that once communicating slows or ceases, it can become very difficult to restart it or make it effective in subsequent phases. If a lapse in communications occurs, the cohesion of the team, relationships with other stakeholders, and control of a project can weaken.

Communications is a subjective process. Although it is important to strive for objectivity, the reality is that communications is fraught with subjectivity. What a project manager decides to communicate, how he or she communicates—this is done in a manner reflecting one's choice and style. Subjectivity highlights what is or is not important to the communicators. The reasons for this subjectivity are not sometimes readily apparent until stakeholders have disagreements over what the project manager has communicated. The choice of medium and technique also reflects the beliefs, values, and preferences of the project manager, and that often lends itself to disagreement.

Ironically, many project managers think that their choice of medium and technique is an objective selection. However, that is not necessarily the case in the minds of others. For that reason alone, they should emphasize the need to apply effective and active listening skills, which are in short supply, and solicit feedback on what they communicate.

Communications requires considerable flexibility and adaptability. Because of the subjective nature of communications, project managers must be willing to maintain an open mind in what and how they choose to communicate. In one phase, for example, a certain medium might work; in another, it may fail dismally. Project managers must assess the context, be flexible, and adapt the medium and technique to achieve their goals and objectives.

Unfortunately, some project managers do not apply flexibility and adaptability in content or approach. What they communicate and how they communicate remind us of how Model Ts were produced on the early production lines: "You can have any color you want as long as it's black." The result is rigidity, with severe consequences. Stakeholders begin to disregard the project manager's messages and start viewing them as administrative nonsense.

The Communications Process

To best understand the communications process, project managers must understand all the relevant factors. First, the communications process requires a sender and receiver. The sender formulates the message to communicate, which is meant for a receiver. The sender crafts the content with some intent in mind. The receiver, of course, receives the message and then deals with it according to personal reactions. He or she may accept, revise, or reject the message. For example, a project manager informs the customer that a slide on a major milestone will occur and provides reasons. The customer, in turn, may make a decision based upon that information.

Second, the communications process requires a medium to communicate the content of a message. The medium may take just about any form, each unique in its ability to influence the receptivity of the receiver. As with the message itself, the receiver may elect to accept or reject the medium employed. The receiver may even elect to alter the medium so that he or she can receive and interpret the message according to his or her preferences. In the earlier example with the schedule slide, a project manager may send the message as e-mail rather than have a face-to-face meeting with the customer.

Third, the communications process requires a message. The message can take many different forms, usually in hard or soft format. The hard format is usually paper whereas soft format is electronic. Regardless of format, a message is necessary to initiate a communication and stimulate a relationship between two or more people. In the aforesaid example, the message is that the project will slide a major milestone and it is sent in a soft (e.g., electronic) format.

Fourth, the communications process requires feedback between the sender and receiver. Feedback may be positive, negative, or neutral, indicating the receptivity of the sender or receiver. Feedback can also be simple or complex. Simple feedback occurs when it involves just two people; complex feedback is when the process involves three or more people. The movement from simple to complex is because the number of channels and opportunities for misinterpretation increase geometrically as each one codes their message and the other decodes the same. In the last example, the customer gives negative feedback in soft copy format but suggests a follow-up meeting to discuss the results.

Fifth, the communications process is rarely "clean," meaning that what the recipient receives may not be necessarily what the sender sent. A number of variables can affect the quality of a message; these include beliefs, values, the emotional impact of a message, and the medium employed. These variables and others, often referred to as "noise," can affect the degree of receptivity of a message and the feedback on the part of the sender or receiver. For example, the sender may not really believe in a message he or she formulates but may be compelled to send it; the content of the message and its mode of delivery may influence the quality of the message and, ultimately, its receptivity. For example, a project manager may decide to communicate via e-mail rather than in person to key stakeholders. The reason may be to avoid direct conflict with the recipients of the message due to the personalities involved.

Sixth, the communications process will always be in a setting, or context, that influences results. This context often involves time, space, and structure. Time may refer to the day of the week. Space may be as simple as the location of a person, or it may involve a project spread over a wide geographical area. Structure may be the organizational network in place for supporting the communications process of a project. For example, a project manager may want to communicate negative information about a schedule performance only in a specific setting, such as a project status review.

Understanding the influence and interplay of the different variables involved requires a deep appreciation of these elements: sender and receiver, message, medium, feedback, variables, and setting.

Sender and Receiver

Communications, like project management, would be easy if not for the personalities involved. All a project manager would have to do is create a message, pick a medium, and send it out. That's it; nothing more.

Communications is not that easy, even if only involving two people. The reality is that senders and receivers are individually as complex as their relationships.

This complexity is reflected in the different thinking styles of people; that is, the way they collect and process information and then respond to it. One tool that reflects this diversity in thinking styles is organizational engineering (OE). OE is a branch of knowledge that seeks understanding, measuring, predicting, and guiding the behavior of groups of people. It does so by considering how people process information and respond to it. By considering both factors, a person's strategic style or pattern of behavior manifests itself over time. OE, of course, is just one of many different typologies that reflect the way people respond to circumstances, which includes communications.

When interactions occur between a sender and receiver, the differences in thinking styles can manifest themselves, offering opportunities for new understandings but also setting the ground for conflicts, some without ultimately positive outcomes.

One effective way to show the relationships and their corresponding complexity is to develop a communications diagram. This diagram shows the interaction in terms of communications exchanges among several people. A line is drawn to indicate who communicates with whom and the information being passed between them. The side benefits of this diagram are that it helps not only to show the "major players" on a project but also to indicate the areas of effective communications and the opportunities for improvement.

A mathematical formula exists to indicate the level of complexity involved on a project from the perspective of communications channels. The formula is simple but adeptly illustrates the complexity behind communications as a number of people are added to a project:

$$[N \times (N - 1)]\ /2, \text{ where N is the number of people on the project}$$

The calculation, of course, tells more than an increase in the number of channels. It reveals the many possibilities in which communications can go awry. If a project is small, say, with 3–5 people, the number can be quite manageable. As the number of people increases, so do the different thinking styles, laying the basis for positive and negative conflict that can build either bridges or walls, respectively, among people. For example, sometimes the management thinks that adding more people on a project will improve project performance, only to get the opposite results. Many times this is due to learning-curve issues; at other times, new people may come aboard who think differently, which can result in conflict that slows progress.

Walls, or barriers, are often overt. These walls include responding incorrectly, not following direction, or distorting the message.

The walls can also be very subtle, intentional or unintentional. The message could be misperceived, for example, from a content or delivery perspective; the receiver could mistrust the sender; or vital data from a message could be omitted, either by design or mistake. For example, a project manager and a stakeholder may have a negative relationship. Information communicated between them can easily be misconstrued because emotions may run high. Many walls can stand in the way of enabling good receptivity toward a message. These walls include body language, phrasing, tool choice, content, cultural differences, timings, and beliefs.

Message

The message is the next important element of the communications process. Without the message, of course, the communications process has no purpose. The message can be categorized.

A message could be informational. Its purpose is to communicate facts and data meaningfully to a recipient. For example, a message might contain status on tasks that a person is responsible to complete.

A message can be persuasive. Its purpose is to persuade one or more persons to act. For example, a message might attempt to persuade people to adopt a new process for reporting status.

A message can entertain. Often, such messages in a project environment are tied closely to informational ones. For example, a message might be an article about stakeholders on a project team having fun during a recent celebration.

A message might be formal or informal. A formal message is documented in both hard and soft copy formats. An informal message tends to arrive through e-mail or word of mouth.

Whether informational, persuasive, or entertaining, a message should follow some very basic guidelines.

A message should communicate clearly. Its purpose should be easily discernible by the receiver and should not contain any confusing verbiage that detracts from its intent. Nothing can cause more confusion and be more tiresome, for example, than to read a lengthy e-mail that has a lot of content, but the reader has to wade through considerable verbiage to determine its purpose.

A message should be concise. Messages should not contain any more words than necessary. Each word should contribute to its purpose and the desired response. For example, if the purpose of a message can be communicated in 20 rather than 200 words, pick the former.

A message should have a logical structure. It should, for example, have content that flows logically, enabling comprehension. The structure of a message usually has an introduction, a body, and concluding statement. Within the body itself the content may be chronological, topical, sequential, or follow some other logical order.

A message should indicate the recipients. Listing the recipients clearly removes any ambiguity over whom the message is intended for and, by consequence, encourages a response.

Finally, a message should contain a request to the recipient to respond, if necessary. By incorporating a request for a response, the receiver acknowledges to the sender receipt of the message.

Medium

The variety of media in today's environment is quite extensive. The media includes face-to-face communications, telephone, voice mail, videoconferencing, television, e-mail and electronic file transmission, radio, and much more.

The choice of the medium for use on a project depends on several factors.

Technological maturity. If the supporting infrastructure exists, all media may be employable. Often, however, that is not the case. The best approach is to employ a variety of media based on the context and desired results. For example, in certain cases a presentation using virtual tools such as Webex may suffice. At other times, an in-person presentation with a stakeholder may prove useful to facilitate greater dialogue and demonstrate the importance of the relationship.

Time. The urgency of sending a message and receiving a response will determine the medium to be employed. Obviously, electronic media can effectively meet this requirement, if the infrastructure exists. If it does not, an alternative medium might suffice, such as a face-to-face meeting. For example, sending an e-mail out to communicate information may prove useful for conveying it quickly rather than waiting for a meeting to be arranged.

Importance. If very important, a face-to-face meeting might prove a most useful medium. For messages of lesser importance, the media might include e-mail, or a few words left on a voice recorder. Often, the importance of a message is demonstrated by the delivery mechanism. Usually, the more personable a message, the greater the impact.

Geography. When the dispersion of the project team members is wider, the electronic medium will often prove more useful and practical than a face-to-face meeting. Videoconferencing and teleconferencing may prove more efficient than an in-person presentation. For example, virtual teams will benefit the most from videoconferencing and teleconferencing.

Custom. Some organizations, and projects within them, may have a preference for using certain media. For example, a face-to-face meeting may be the preferred choice for people who are used to working together in a single location. Other organizations and their projects may prefer e-mail as the primary means of communication, reserving meetings for rare occasions.

Impact. If a project manager desires a high impact from his or her messages, a face-to-face meeting may be more preferable than simply sending an e-mail, one of many lost in a sea of e-mails. Again, the general rule is that the more personable the approach, the greater the impact.

Content. The more the desired impact of content, the greater the importance in choosing the most appropriate medium. Communications that requires direct, ongoing exchange of messages necessitate employing face-to-face meetings or electronic media, such as video-conferencing. For example, the more interactive the content, the greater the impact. That is why tools like Instant Messenger have become quite popular.

Receptivity. Some messages may prove controversial or generate fear, and the choice of the medium can either increase or decrease the level of receptivity. Usually, the less emotion surrounding a message, the less the medium matters. Paper documents tend to cool down a message, where as most electronic messages, such as e-mail, heat things up due to its immediacy. For example, a project manager reports a low schedule performance index (SPI) for a section of the schedule and sends out the results in a broadcast e-mail message. This approach will get greater visibility than if the results were placed on a few hard copies and then filed in a drawer somewhere.

Feedback. Movies, television transmission, and compact discs communicating a message provide less opportunity for feedback than meetings and e-mail. If a sender places critical importance on feedback, then a more personal approach may be preferable. In-person presentations, such as project status meetings, will generate substantial feedback, especially if the dialogue is open.

Obstacles. If the obstacles are widespread and intense, then the sender may elect to employ a series of physical or electronic meetings to encourage feedback. If not, then more general "broadcasting" media, such as television or e-mail, might suffice. Obstacles can take many forms to include limited time, space, money, and energy, as well as people's attitudes, motivations, and paradigms.

Trust and credibility. If the level of trust and credibility is low, the sender may elect to use a medium that encourages a more personal interchange with the receiver. In some cases, however, personal approaches may not work well because the level of credibility and trust may be low among stakeholders.

Formality or informality. Usually, a higher degree of formality is associated with importance; consequently, less formality accompanies messages of less importance. More formal approaches include large meetings requiring physical presence, broadcast videoconference sessions, and e-mail links to Web sites, which reflect greater formality than holding a teleconferencing or telecom session.

Quantity. When there is more data and less information, then computing is more preferable than teleconferencing for transferring the content. Massive quantities of data and information must be handled very carefully to avoid overload, loss, and misinterpretation. Sometimes, the use of automated scheduling tools, for example, can tend to spew more data and information than anyone ever imagined. The amount can be so overwhelming that many people will seek other sources to keep them informed about their project.

Quality. If a message is more "casual" in content, for example, it is nice to use, a less formal medium such as an e-mail. However, if quality matters, such as the appearance or desired emotional impact, then selection is important. For high visibility material, a project manager may consider a formal presentation to convey information rather than sending e-mail. Formal display of output usually connotes something of critical importance and demands attention.

Communications infrastructure. A linear structure for an organization will often involve more sequential and time-consuming approaches, for example, sending a chain e-mail or hard copy document; a hierarchical structure will require a broadcast medium, such as satellite broadcast. In today's environment, linear structures are rare because of e-mail. However, it can be done in cases where a select group of people need to review the e-mail before it is broadcast to the entire organization. For example, a project announcement may be reviewed by a few executives before it is sent as a broadcast message throughout an organization.

Thinking styles. Some receivers, for example, do not process narrative text very well. Others are more visually oriented. Senders need to consider the predominant thinking styles of their recipients to increase receptivity and obtain the desired responses. For example, some people have a preference for drawings, diagrams, and other graphics to communicate. Others prefer narrative text.

Of course, project managers use some or all of the determinants to select a medium. None of the above solely determines a selection. They do so by weighing them from the perspective of their goals, the audience, and the desired results.

Feedback

Sending a message from a sender to a receiver through a medium is important, but not enough. Feedback is equally important. Without feedback, a sender has no idea whether he or she is effective or not.

Feedback can be either positive or negative. Positive feedback is associated with confirmation by the receiver that he or she has received and understood the message. Negative feedback indicates that a receiver did not receive or understand a message.

Most project managers prefer positive acceptance. Often, positive acceptance reflects a good working relationship with recipients. However, positive feedback may have bad consequences for a project. The person providing the feedback may indicate he or she reflects some degree of groupthink. In other words, positive feedback may not be genuine. Many times some people find it hard to communicate negative feedback for fear of rejection or retaliation. They have a tendency to prepare the feedback in a manner that the project manager may not find meaningful or can't even understand.

Negative feedback may provide value. It may indicate, ironically, credibility and trust between the sender and receiver. If a response is very negative, it may provide an opportunity to increase dialogue and trust between both parties. Ironically, negative feedback may, if handled correctly, serve as a springboard for generating change. It can force issues into the open that would enable people to exchange thoughts and generate solutions. The challenge is in getting the sender and receiver to be open with each other.

The best approach for handling feedback is for the sender to verify that the recipient has received the message as intended and for the receiver to verify the intent. This mutuality regarding feedback can help ensure that a message is not misconstrued and that the sender receives valuable feedback from the recipient. It is dangerous to assume that a message, even when articulated well, has been understood by the recipient. A simple word choice can spark emotions that cause all receptivity to any thought or action to cease.

Obtaining feedback is very difficult because the communications process is ambiguous. The common perception is that it is merely two people communicating, such as over a telephone line; however, more than just an on or off response is occurring between a sender and receiver. Rather, there are factors to consider that can interfere with a message being "pinged" back and forth.

An arc of distortion occurs between the sender and receiver and it plays a prominent role in feedback. This arc, from a figurative perspective, can stretch to varying lengths and consist of different contents. It influences the difference between what the sender intends to communicate and what the recipient receives. The greater the length of the arc, the greater the chance of message distortion.

Basically, the arc of distortion is the "noise" affecting a message. The content and length of the arc can substantially impact the quality of feedback between the sender and receiver. Cognitive factors, such as paradigms, consisting of an array of beliefs and values, color perceptions of reality. These paradigms can largely influence what messages a person perceives, what he or she deems important, and how he or she responds or reacts. The arc of distortion involves and influences the sender and receiver. Both choose what is important from their individual perspectives. Each perspective affects feedback both in quality and quantity of material and the choice of response. All of this is interrelated and compounded with distance, timing, attention span, and language.

Distance. The greater the distance between the sender and receiver, the greater the likelihood that the receiver might not receive the entire message or might misinterpret it. A signal may become attenuated over a long distance; so can a message. When a message is sent over a long distance, the chances for miscommunication and viewing it as less important can increase. This situation is often the case with global projects. Although a message may be clear and concise, the connotation, as opposed to the denotation, may distort its understanding and importance.

Timing. The content of the message may ordinarily appear neutral but at a particular moment in time, it may cause a negative reaction by a recipient. The most famous example, of course, is presenting your manager with bad news on Monday morning or late Friday afternoon when normally that information is insignificant. In general, a good time rarely exists for giving negative feedback. What is important is the context when negative feedback is provided. Timing is one of the contextual factors that can influence how well a stakeholder receives negative feedback.

Selective attention. The sender may communicate a message that the receiver does not deem important or does not want to hear. The "Tell me what I want to hear and not what I need to hear" scenario is a typical example in some project environments. This circumstance is more common than one might imagine. Many project managers may find dealing with executive stakeholders so overwhelming that they might adjust the data and information to downplay the importance of the message.

Language. Choosing and interpreting words can impact feedback. Semantics, the meaning of words, can greatly impact communications among two or more people. Words can be either detonative or connotative. The former deals with the literal interpretation of a word; the latter deals with its subjective nature. Connotative interpretation can have a significant influence on feedback. If a sender chooses a word that he or she thinks is innocuous, the recipient may have the opposite perception.

Variables

When considering the immense complexity surrounding the communications process, it is amazing that people understand one another at all. The number of variables seem endless. Yet, some are basic:

Beliefs and values. These variables have a prominent influence on the communications process. There are, however, several others.

Body language. The study of body language is often referred to as *kinesics*. The sender and receiver exhibit body language, which includes gestures, eye movement, and facial expressions. Three major keys to understanding and mastering the study of body language are to consider words, actions, and environmental context.

The best approach for interpreting body language is to apply the principle of congruency, that is, determining whether the body language is synchronized with words spoken. In other words, whether the body language re-enforces what is or is not said. For example, a project manager may say that he wants to listen to team members, but his arms crisscross his chest while others speak.

Eye contact is another important part of body language. Indirect eye contact may indicate inattentiveness. Looking out the window, for example, while someone talks indicates that attention is elsewhere.

Vocal considerations, too, are important. Factors such as volume, rate, and pitch, indicate a person's degree of engagement in communicating. Rapidity in speech can reflect one's interest level.

The environment, of course, can have an impact. In a cold room, for example, crossing one's arms may indicate a desire to get warm, or defensiveness, or a person's natural physical behavior. Environmental factors can interfere, therefore, with interpretation. The challenge is to discern the psychological motives behind the body language. Congruency and context are keys for making the correct interpretation.

Language is also an important variable. Language is more complex to interpret than body language because so much is involved in choosing and mixing words. Semantics is about the meaning of words. Words can have a literal or symbolic meaning, or both. *Detonative* is the term for describing the literal meaning of a word and *connotative,* the subjective meaning. Detonative definitions relate more to intellectual, whereas connotative more cognitive, beliefs associated with a word and its corresponding affective or emotional qualities. Neither detonation nor connotation is more important than the other. However, connotation often has greater impact. For example, the choice of a word describing the state of a project, although accurate, may have "emotional baggage" or positive connotations.

The number of variables and their relationships are immense in quantity and quality. However, some basic heuristics can be employed.

First, reciprocity is important. Two or more people must have a willingness to engage in an open exchange. If the recipient and sender alike are unwilling to exchange messages to any varying degree, communications fails. For example, two team members may feel considerable animosity toward each other. Although one of them may have a valid point, the recipient may not listen, let alone hear.

Second, all exchanges will involve some degree of action and reaction. Action is taking the initiative by the sender to send a message; reaction is responding to the message, positively, neutrally, or negatively. This interchange can occur several times in one or more multiple ways. For example, two or more team members may not want to share information due to mutual distrust. One person denies another person's repeated request for data, regardless of importance.

Third, congruent and incongruent behaviors play important roles in feedback. The sender and receiver "watch" each other to ensure that his or her behavior matches both what is communicated and the manner in which communications occur. If a sender or recipient fails to meet perceptions and expectations, the feedback suffers. For example, a team member may feel another person lacks the background to discuss a subject intelligently. The former might disregard any insight, regardless of merit.

Fourth, a feedback process occurs explicitly and implicitly. A sender and recipient may communicate their degree of receptiveness overtly. Or, they may communicate subtly, reflected in acting and reacting to a message. For example, a recipient of an e-mail responds to a "flame," or negative message. The person receiving the e-mail responds in the same manner, and the situation escalates.

Fifth, feedback involves the sender and recipient operating on assumptions, because the information they possess is incomplete or inaccurate. Assumptions can make it very difficult to guarantee the specific affects and effects of a message. About the only way to confirm the effectiveness of a message is by giving attention to intentional, even unintentional results. For example, a team member makes an inadvertent comment about the quality of a deliverable to another person. The latter assumes that the person speaking is attacking him or her.

Setting

The setting involves three variables that exist in any environment that can influence the quantity and quality of feedback: time, space, and structure.

Time. The more time available, the greater the opportunity for better communications to exist up to a point. If the content and approach toward communications are flawed, then, of course, the amount of time makes little difference. Generally, however, the more time available, the better the communications. Greater attention can be spent on encoding and decoding messages and developing effective responses. Too little time lends itself to knee-jerk reactions and making mistakes. Of course, this generally applies to the processing of messages.

When transmitting a message, however, less time is better. Less transmission time means more currency and relevancy of content. Taking too long to communicate a message may obviate the value of the content, because circumstances could change.

Space. The greater the geographical distance between senders and recipients, the greater the chances that the content will lose value and have emotional impact due to a lack of immediacy. Content loses value if considerable time is required for a message to travel, thereby reducing its value to a recipient. It loses its emotional impact because the immediacy may not exist; to a certain extent, the message becomes an abstraction. For example, a message sent over a geographically dispersed team may not have effect on some recipients due to their distant locations as opposed to someone closer to the originator of the message.

Structure. Structure very much reflects time and space. Structure manifests itself in the form of networks, usually consisting of nodes and links. The architecture of these nodes and links reflects how communications in general and

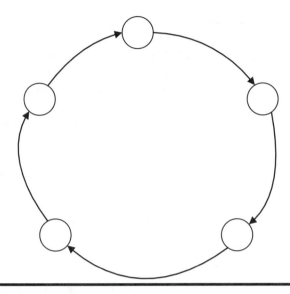

Figure 1.4   Circle network.

feedback in particular occur. Nodes reflect entities, such as people, organizations, or equipment; links reflect the relationships of the nodes as avenues of communication. Four forms of networks exist: wheel, linear, hierarchical, and relational.

The circle or wheel network (Figures 1.4 and 1.5) is in the form of a circle with nodes forming a ring. Communications flows from one node to the next, relaying a message from one node to the next, until it reaches its intended recipient. An example is a message being sent from one person to the next. A variant of the circle is the cartwheel, whereby one node serves as a "traffic cop" with responsibility for regulating the quantity and quality of transmissions. An example is a project manager sends a message to each recipient and reviews the responses before sending it to another person.

The linear network (Figure 1.6) is in the form of a straight line, with each node sequentially falling one after another. Communications flows from one node to the next until a message reaches its intended recipient. An example is a serial review of a message, whereby one recipient reviews it first and then forwards it on to the next one.

A variant of a linear network is the Y network (Figure 1.7), whereby one node serves as a traffic cop with responsibility for regulating the quantity and quality of communications. An example is a serial review of a message until it reaches a specific recipient, who then determines which subsequent ones receive it.

The wheel and linear networks are simple and frequently exist in the project environment. A problem with both is that a failure by one node can bring the

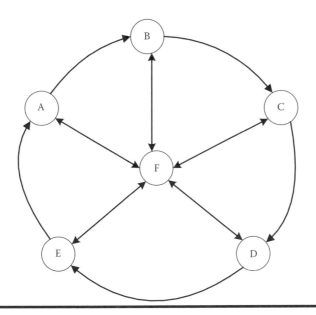

Figure 1.5 Wheel network.

Figure 1.6 Linear network.

communications network to a standstill. The virtue of the networks is their simplicity—until the number of nodes and the corresponding links increase.

A hierarchical network (Figure 1.8) reflects a top–down or bottom–up communications flow. The nodes are arranged hierarchically, whereby some nodes are more important than others. A hierarchical network reflects more of an organization chart, with the higher nodes having more importance than the lower ones. A message often flows linearly but can do so via multiple paths. Although the flow can be bidirectional, meaning flowing both up and down a path, often the flow is unidirectional—more down than up. Hierarchical networks are more versatile than linear and wheel networks because they have multiple links. However, if the "top" node fails, communications suffers. An example is when the top node, such as a project manager, sends a message with the expectation of receiving no feedback.

A relational network (Figure 1.9) consists of a patchwork of nodes, each one having a series of links. The architecture of the nodes and links is analogous to neural networks, whereby each cell (akin to a node) has multiple synapses (akin to links) to other cells. Although the structure appears complex in comparison to the wheel and linear networks, the reality is that the relational network provides more

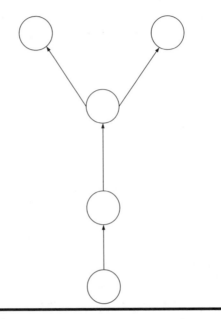

Figure 1.7 Y network.

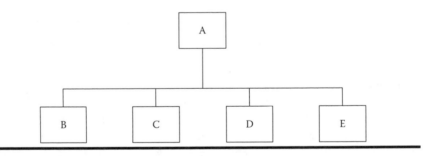

Figure 1.8 Hierarchical network.

versatility and adaptability when one or the other nodes crash. Communications does not rely simply on a chief node. An example is when a node, such as a project manager, relays a message to multiple recipients, but does not control its flow.

The trend in communications in general and feedback in particular is to strive to institute relational networks. The combination of efficient and effective communications technology, a greater awareness of information as a valuable asset, and the development of data repositories all make relational networks a practical approach to be applied in business environments, especially on projects.

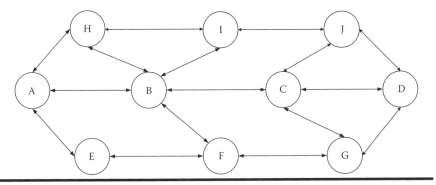

Figure 1.9   Relational network.

At the Center

The principal vehicle for enabling effective communications on a project is the PMIS (Figure 1.10). At the core, the PMIS is the repository consisting of data and information relevant to the project. To be useful, the content of the repository must be accessible, organized, current, and meaningful.

Stakeholders in general and project managers in particular use the repository to perform key communications functions. These key functions are:

■ Applying active and effective listening
■ Preparing a communications management plan and establishing an issues management process
■ Drafting and publishing documentation

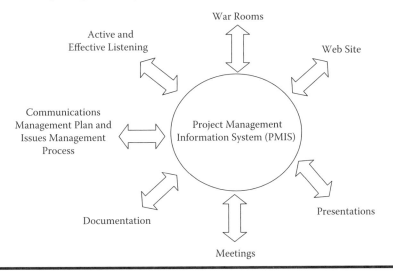

Figure 1.10   PMIS and project communications management skills.

- Conducting meetings
- Giving effective presentations
- Developing and deploying a Web site
- Building war rooms

Of course, each project manager has his or her particular style when communicating; what they choose to communicate, when, where, why, and how, all reflective of their personality. The source for enabling them to communicate uniquely according to their personality is the PMIS.

A Difficult Process

Communicating effectively does not come easily. Project managers serve as linchpins on their projects. They are the only ones who must communicate with all stakeholders. To do so effectively, they must use considerable discretion in the approaches and techniques that they apply to their unique circumstances. If they succeed as communicators, then the likelihood of their success increases. If they communicate poorly, the likelihood is that their projects will have poor results.

References

1. Speakup. *PM Network*, October 2006, p. 6.
2. Peter Fretty. Why Do Projects Really Fail? *PM Network*, March 2006, p. 48.
3. Top 10 Project Management Challenges. *PM Network*, April 2004, p. 18.
4. Sarah F. Gale. Clear Channels. *PM Network*, September 2005, p. 62.
5. Marianne K. McGee. The Useless Hunt for Data. *Informationweek*, January 8, 2007, p. 19.
6. Edward Prewitt. Why IT Leaders Fail. *CIO*, August 1, 2005, p. 22.

Getting Started Checklist		
Question	*Yes*	*No*
1. When you send out messages, do you consider these elements carefully:		
Feedback?		
Medium?		
Message?		
Sender and receiver?		
Setting or context?		
2. What category of message do you usually send:		
Entertaining?		
Informational?		
Persuasive?		
3. Do your messages typically have these qualities:		
Clear?		
Concise?		
Defined recipients?		
Formal?		
Informal?		
Logical?		
Specific feedback?		
4. Whatever communications that you select for sending your message, do you consider:		
Communications infrastructure?		
Content?		
Custom?		
Feedback?		
Formality or informality?		
Geography?		
Impact?		
Importance?		
Obstacles?		
Quality?		
Quantity?		
Receptivity?		
Technological maturity?		

Getting Started Checklist (Continued)		
Question	*Yes*	*No*
Thinking styles?		
Time?		
Trust and credibility?		
5. Did you consider that these factors might affect the communications process in general:		
Beliefs and values?		
Body language?		
Distance?		
Language?		
Selective attention?		
Semantics?		
Timing?		
6. Did you consider that these variables might affect quality of feedback:		
Assumptions of sender and receiver?		
Congruent and incongruent behavior?		
Explicit and implicit responses?		
Reciprocity?		
The degree of action and reaction?		
7. Did you consider these factors regarding the setting of the communications:		
Space?		
Structure?		
Time?		
8. For the structure, did you identify one of these communications networks to use:		
Circle network?		
Hierarchical network?		
Linear network?		
Relational network?		
Wheel network?		
Y network?		

Chapter 2

Establishing the Project Management Information System

The concept of a project management information system, or PMIS, is an important component of project communications management. A PMIS is an effective mechanism for enabling and facilitating communications. All processes and activities on a project center on it because the success of a project depends as much on the quality of data as it does on completing the works on time and within budget. Indeed, a persuasive argument can be made that if the PMIS fails or the quality of its basic elements does not meet a certain standard, then the likelihood of project failure from a cost, schedule, or quality perspective will increase. Accepting this argument means that establishing a PMIS is absolutely critical.

Definition and Components

A PMIS is an integrated, interdependent set of processes, activities, techniques, and data used to define, plan, control, execute, and close a project to achieve optimum performance regarding cost, schedule, and quality.

The best approach to understanding a PMIS is to view it as a data-intensive system. A PMIS has several components.

The most important one, of course, is the *repository*, comprising data and information about a project. This data may be stored manually or electronically and provides various levels of access to the people needing it. It is important to note that the repository is more than just the database for a scheduling package. It also contains other data about a project, from a copy of the charter to a change management log.

Another component, especially if data is stored electronically, is the *technology* to support it. This component can consist of hardware, such as servers, and software, for example, a database management system (DBMS). This technology requires constant updating because of the rapid pace of development. However, the right hardware and software, provided training is available, can increase the power of a PMIS.

Methodology is another key component of a PMIS. A project management methodology determines—even dictates—the business rules for storing, accessing, and addressing a data repository under specific conditions. It can prove, however, to be an asset or a liability to a PMIS. For example, the rules of the methodology may be so detailed and cumbersome that people will not visit the repository, resulting in their taking short cuts by circumventing the PMIS.

Policies and procedures are important components. They may go beyond the methodology, reflecting the requirements of a larger organizational infrastructure much greater than a project. Still, they may influence the deployment of a PMIS and its access for specific business reasons. An example is a companywide policy or procedure restricting certain project data and information from contractors.

Stakeholders are also important components. They, of course, are people or organizations having an interest in the outcome of a project. Many of the stakeholders, to varying degrees, will have an interest in using the PMIS to satisfy their own requirements.

Forms and reports are critical components. Forms are used, of course, to collect data to populate the PMIS. Reports are necessary to provide information in a format and level of detail that satisfies the needs and wants of a stakeholder. The complication with forms is that sometimes they are used to collect more data than necessary; the complication with reports is that they sometimes generate more data than information.

The *principles, techniques, and tools of project management* are components that are often overlooked. Yet, they vary from one environment to another and from one organization to the next. These principles, techniques, and tools will influence the quantity and quality of data in the PMIS.

The *environment*, or context, is an often overlooked as a component of a PMIS. It can have a substantial influence on whether a PMIS will be deployable and how it will be deployed. Business conditions, management style, historical approaches toward managing projects, and available funding can influence the extent to which a PMIS will be deployed and utilized.

Key Characteristics

An efficient and effective PMIS possesses certain characteristics.

Integration is a key behavior. Each component plays an important role in converting data into information to satisfy the requirements of a project. If a component fails, then the usefulness of output may be lacking.

Interdependence is another key behavior. This depends on the transmission and sharing of data to produce information for the stakeholders on a project. The shortcomings or failure by one component can influence the performance of a PMIS. For example, a schedule based upon incorrect data can lead to stakeholders making decisions that may have negative long-term impact on the service or product being delivered to the customer.

The overall pattern of behavior of a PMIS is reflected in the degree of integration and interdependence of its components. A more complex PMIS, reflected in the terms of quantity and relationships among components, will have a more sophisticated pattern of behavior than one with fewer components and relationships. More complexity often equates better performance, but it also can result in more dramatic impacts when breakdowns occur.

Activities performed by a PMIS include retrieving data from different sources, sending information to specific destinations, transforming or transmitting data and information (or both), storing data and information, and providing controls over the access and disbursal of data and information. The execution of these activities often reflects the degree of integration and interdependence among the components of a PMIS. For large projects, the relationship of these activities can be quite complex. Different applications and equipment may be involved, which requires, for instance, restricting certain access rights to systems and data to external partners. Such circumstances can add a level of complexity to the integration and interdependence of a PMIS for a project.

Data, of course, plays an important role in ensuring integration and interdependence. Indeed, it is the "blood" that permeates and nourishes a PMIS. It must be supplied or acquired, compiled, processed, "packaged," and then delivered to the appropriate recipient in the form of information. The information, in turn, is then utilized by the recipient. All of this occurs systematically. Data collected from different sources, such as project leads, for example, is sent to distributed servers and applications and, in turn, is sent to a central repository for processing. The data at the central repository is processed to calculate cost and schedule progress for each area of responsibility. The information is then returned back to the originators for further decision making. This is often the scenario for projects with activities spread across a wide geographical area.

The information generated by these activities is reflected on the many information-sharing events that occur on a project, which include the conducting of meetings, giving presentations, listening actively and effectively, producing documentation, deploying a project Web site, and setting up a war room.

Roles

Nevertheless, PMIS activities could never occur without involving the stakeholders who need it. Tom Davenport has identified several important roles from an ecological perspective, and they are stakeholders. The roles are data producers, custodians, and consumers; information suppliers; manufacturers; consumers; and product managers.

Data producers are stakeholders who create data to eventually populate the repository such as project managers and team members. Data custodians are the people such as project planners and data analysts, who manage the repository and the supporting infrastructure. Data consumers are the stakeholders who use the data in some way, such as generating cost and schedule reports. Information suppliers compile information that is generated (such as planners and schedulers). Information manufacturers perform a similar role as the data custodians (such as data analysts) by providing sufficient support for the project. Information consumers are the people who use information for their activities (such as project managers and executive stakeholders). Product managers, such as scheduling tool experts, oversee the overall process of capturing and storing data as well as producing and distributing information.

Some stakeholders may perform multiple roles. For example, a project manager might be a data producer, information producer, and information product manager at the same time or at different points in time; the same role assumption can occur for other stakeholders.

Developing an Automated PMIS

In most environments, a PMIS is usually automated to a certain extent using information technology (Figure 2.1)

First, hardware is necessary, ranging anywhere from a stand-alone PC to several servers networked together to provide storage, access, and print capabilities for stakeholders. Some servers function as dedicated data servers and others as print servers, for example, while multiple users share a server.

Second, software is necessary, deploying one or more applications to capture data and generate reports. These applications can reside on a stand-alone PC, a server, or a combination of both. User site licenses are common for applications, particularly for applications used by multiple workstations.

Additional software items are DBMS to manage access, storage, and distribution of data. Several varieties of DBMS exist, but the most common is the relational database management system (RDMS), which allows access and update of data and information using a structured query language (SQL). Under some circumstances, a DBMS might support spatial and object-oriented data structures.

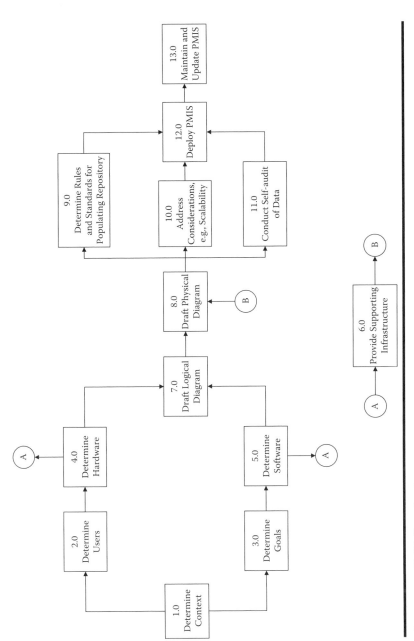

Figure 2.1 PMIS flowchart.

Logical and physical designs are developed to reflect the overall architecture of the servers and the partitioning of software and data among those servers. Logical designs concentrate on how all the hardware, software, and data interact; physical designs display how all three are physically allocated. Often, physical and logical designs are developed separately for hardware, software, and data, although they can be combined into a composite logical and physical design.

In today's environment, because of a highly networked environment, middleware becomes an important consideration. Middleware may involve such standards as Common Oriented Request Broker Architecture (CORBA) and Distributed Computing Environment (DCE), for example, which enable an open computing environment.

There are a number of considerations to address when developing and deploying an automated PMIS.

Scalability is important. This consideration deals with the potential growth in the use and application of a PMIS. A key question is whether, over time, the growth in use and data storage can bring the PMIS down, or crash. Of more concern is whether a PMIS implementation has the potential for "code, load, and explode" scenario.

Portability is a key consideration. Will it be able to function on different platforms, for example, in a microcomputer or minicomputer? Will it also be run on different operating systems?

Access is another important consideration. Some data and information may be accessible only to a few people although just about everyone connected to a project will want access. An administrator is often assigned the control of access to the resources of a PMIS.

Data representation is important, too. Content and structure of the data residing in a PMIS are important to enable the efficient and effective use of resources to perform calculations and reporting. A logical data model can go a long way in helping to understand the content and structure of a PMIS. It also enables better coding and employing software agents to ensure notification and automated corrective action of program performance problems.

Data Versus Information

Typically, project managers and other project management professionals focus their energies too narrowly on time.

Time is a very subjective concept, regardless of a manager's need to produce on schedule. A worker's sense of time varies considerably from one person to the next and from one culture to another. For example, a global project involves people of various nationalities. Different nationalities give varying importance to time and a project, such as low time is spent *vis-à-vis* the United States.

Yet, the temptation exists to treat time as some objective criterion universally, although precision is far from the norm in predicting project performance anywhere. Time for a project is often either over- or underestimated, rarely hitting the mark. The primary reason for dismal time performance on projects is unrealistic expectations based on insufficient of data and information.

Despite the flood of data and information in our lives in general, and on specific projects in particular, the right amount of data and information in the right format at the right time is often in short supply. A PMIS often becomes an anachronism in a project environment, and the content, a mismatch with reality.

Environmental conditions change constantly, outpacing the ability to capture enough data quickly. Dynamic capture of data and churning it into useful information does not occur fast enough. For example, for a fast-paced project under a tight schedule, the frequency of updates to a repository may prove crucial for making decisions; batch collection and processing of data may not suffice. Stakeholders may not have the patience to wait for a tool to generate the information that they need to make a decision.

A PMIS may well become a "garbage bin" of data. The result is that access to the right data and information becomes too difficult, requiring users to wade, or drill down, to the content that they need or want. A common misfortune of technology-intensive projects is that data is collected for data's sake. People may, for example, feed data into a repository that satisfies the requirements of a scheduling tool with needless content that has no use, or, they may have to burrow through needless data to obtain the information they need.

These conditions can have severe consequences, which can negatively impact project performance. Data smog is one. Lack of qualitative data obscures efforts to generate clear and reliable information. Stakeholders subsequently exhibit confusion over the output and are unclear about the information generated. A perfect example are reports on cost and schedule going to people who neither have a care or a need for them.

Attention deficit is another consequence. If a PMIS contains too much irrelevant data and produces too much information, then fewer people will pay attention to the output. Quite often, in the age of computers, the problem is too much data and information, and not too little. A commonplace situation is that the custodians of this technology often generate so many varieties of reports that eventually people begin to ignore the output, a phenomenon akin to a loss of hearing from exposure to too much noise. Consequently, little or no data may have value to the stakeholders.

Information overload can also occur. What is generated from a PMIS may be so voluminous that no one may be able to use and interpret the output. In other words, overload may be reflective of too much of a good thing, rendering it absolutely useless. Output, for example, from a scheduling tool may be so voluminous that stakeholders may find it difficult to get the information that they need. The volume may be so great that it is analogous to trying to find a needle in a haystack.

Allied with information overload is the tendency to rush to judgment. A rush to judgment is really an expression of frustration with an unmanageable amount of content or flowed data. For example, the amount of data supporting the information in a scheduling report may be so great that a few stakeholders, like the project manager or executive sponsor, may find it frustrating to try to understand how a value was derived. Instead, they simply focus on one or two indicators, such as the schedule performance index (SPI) or cost performance index (CPI), and ignore all other values. Hence, the need to simplify may result in only partially understanding a report.

All of these consequences can lead to dissatisfaction with a PMIS and a high level of distrust toward output. However, the results are even more devastating. It can lead to flawed decisions by key stakeholders, lower morale, and can increase costs that translate into schedule slippage, budget overruns, and rework.

Populating and maintaining a PMIS can prove, therefore, quite challenging. What many project managers and other stakeholders fail to realize is that the dumping of too much data and information increases the impact of flaws.

As information relies on data, the relationship between the two is highly sensitive and symbiotic. This relationship becomes clear when "tainted" data is used to generate information. Garbage in, garbage out (GIGO) is a perfect example of this challenge. Bad data in a repository inevitably results in incorrect information being incorporated in cost and schedule reports. Initial bad data can corrupt the entire chain of events.

Data redundancy can be a serious problem. Data that is replicated in a repository not only consumes unnecessary resources (for example, disk space), it can also lead to double counting. Duplicate data can cause, for example, exaggeration in values reflected in a cost report, often negatively. Even something as simple as putting a decimal point in the wrong position in a data field can skew the resulting information.

Data inconsistency is another problem. For example, if not stored in a consistent format, it may be counted many times or be overlooked. Establishing metadata rules is a good way to deal with this circumstance.

Incorrect or incomplete data naturally can lead to incorrect information. Incorrect, or "bad" data has a tendency to propagate like a virus, infecting everything. Cleansing data upfront is critical to avoiding corrupting results generated from a repository. Validation of input data plays an important role, too, to ensure, for example, no transposition has occurred. A repository should incorporate good data-entry controls to ensure that data inconsistency is minimal. These controls include range and format checks.

Irrelevant data can pose problems. Although the data may not be included in generating information, it does consume resources, often a considerable amount. It is important, therefore, to check the repository periodically to determine the relevancy of data. Irrelevant data can slow down the performance of a system and consume valuable server space. Project managers should periodically audit the contents of the repository for relevance and purge it. Irrelevant data can also show up in reports, which can only add to the confusion. A periodic data purge can help ensure that the output remains relevant to stakeholders.

Data bias is another problem. Selecting data for a repository may be prejudiced, often reflecting one's preferences. For example, only data that is slanted in a certain direction is entered into a repository. This slanted data propagates and is used for decision making. Of course, this challenge is as much a question of ethics as it is one of accuracy. Project managers and other custodians of a PMIS must always question the accuracy and reliability of the data that is entered into the repository. This skepticism is the best preventive medicine for ensuring that biased data does not enter into a PMIS.

Discovering all the errors discussed above at the wrong point in time can prove challenging. For example, if rules to populate a repository are undefined upfront, the quality of information decreases. If the credibility of the data weakens, so will that of a PMIS.

Keeping these challenges in mind is important not just for credibility but for another reason: a sort of "Gresham's Law of Data" exists. Just as bad money weeds out good, so does bad data. When bad data becomes the norm rather than the exception, which can happen easily, fewer people will be inclined to use PMIS when managing their projects. Perhaps the biggest threat to the usability of a PMIS is the loss of credibility in the output. If stakeholders do not believe the reports, for example, then the value and use of a PMIS will decline dramatically. Stakeholders will find alternative ways to find the status of a project.

It is quite clear that project managers should make every effort to ensure that data is timely, accurate, complete, and consistent. Just as important, they should ensure that data satisfies the fitness of use criteria to ensure that the right of amount of data and its quality is dependent on context. An information-intensive project, for example, should ensure that only relevant, meaningful data populates the repository so that stakeholders receive the information they need responsively and flexibly. At the same time, project managers must ensure that a PMIS in general, and its repository in particular, is scalable to satisfy growing and expanding needs and wants.

To maintain the value of a PMIS, project managers should be vigilant by capturing and investigating complaints, and monitoring the performance of a PMIS. A key question to ask is: Are stakeholders receiving the information they need in the right format at the right time and place? A negative answer to that question necessitates an investigation and action to ensure necessary corrections.

If a challenge surrounding the quality and quantity of data and information persists, project managers may find it necessary to conduct a self-audit of a PMIS. A process-oriented audit works best to determine the exact source of a problem and to avoid the "blame game" that can arise on a project.

Conducting a self-audit may be best done by looking at the different categories of data that Tom Davenport has identified. The first category is known as data views—that is, the model or models that exist to capture data. These models influence what is selected as data and how it is viewed as data. The second category is data values, dealing with issues like accuracy and consistency. The third category is presentation, looking at the format and interpretation of data. The final category is administrative, pertaining to topics like security and ownership of data.

Building a good process model of the flow of data on a project can provide helpful insights on identifying the essential who, what, when where, why, and how of converting data into information. These models, usually in the form of maps or diagrams, can depict quite accurately the capture and process of data, and the output of information into reports.

By looking at each of these four categories from an integrated perspective, project managers and other team members can identify the causes of bad data, for example, propagating throughout a PMIS. This self-audit is best achieved by systemically looking at the sources of data, the processes using it, and the destinations of information. A total perspective can then identify which controls must exist to alleviate or eradicate a problem by actions like cleansing data, which improves the reliability and credibility of information produced by a PMIS.

Types of Repositories

The breadth of a PMIS can be either broad or narrow in coverage, the former being a warehouse and the latter, a data mart.

A PMIS may be a data warehouse, being populated with data from different operational systems. The warehouse enables users of the PMIS to generate the information for their reports. The coverage is broad because it may include, for example, data that covers technical and business topics.

It may also be a data mart, which is a more narrow coverage of a topic. A data mart may include scheduling or financial data but not engineering data, for example. The population of the data may be fed from an operational system. Whether using a warehouse or data mart, stakeholders using a PMIS will have to perform certain activities to ensure the content remains useful.

An activity already mentioned is data cleansing. It requires extracting the necessary data in a way to ensure that the "impurities" do not propagate into any information. On many projects, data entered into a repository may contain all sorts of errors, such as transposition and transcription errors, or may be inconsistent with prescribed procedures. It can be as simple as incorrect content in a report that happens to reside in the repository, which could be used to reconstruct an audit trail.

Data mining is an activity. Stakeholders, using their knowledge of the relationships and patterns associated with the data in a repository, generate their information. In the contemporary environment, stakeholders often have the ability to access data and pull the information that they need. This ability, of course, requires having adequate security controls to ensure people have the access privileges that they need, yet with restricted abilities to modify the database.

Another activity is visualizing and reporting the results of queries. Stakeholders must have the ability to take information and produce it in a meaningful format. These formats might include tabular reports, charts, and diagrams. Stakeholders have different preferences for seeing information. Some people prefer a visual format, whereas others like a compact form, such as a matrix. Powerful data query tools are available that enable stakeholders to generate the reports that they need without the aid of an information technology specialist.

Data replication is another important activity. It is critical that stakeholders ensure that the repository is populated from other systems at the right point in time to attain relevancy of content with no loss of credibility. A critical step is to ensure that the operational systems feed a repository with the most recent information for accurate visualization and reporting. This situation is especially critical for projects that span multiple time zones across the globe. The timing of updates of a repository must be synchronized so that the reports do not reflect incompleteness or incorrectness.

Keys to Making a PMIS Meaningful

For a PMIS to meaningfully contribute to the success of a project, it must have specific characteristics.

A *PMIS must provide the right amount of data and information* in the right format and at the right level of detail. In other words, it must provide both in a manner that satisfies the needs and wants of each stakeholder. With today's technology and the spread of information technology, a PMIS should satisfy this requirement to a certain degree. The days of just pumping out data and information to stakeholders is long past. Software applications allow for greater sophistication in drilling for and displaying content that satisfies the needs of stakeholders. A PMIS, coupled with the latest tools, can meet the needs of most stakeholders.

It must allow access to data and information to the people needing it. Accessibility means people confronting as little resistance to acquire the data and information that they need. Any administrative requirements, for example, must minimize efforts to gain access. In fact, an argument can be made that requirements should enhance rather than restrict access. Increasingly, stakeholders are expecting access to more data and information than ever before. Thanks to improved data mining tools and techniques, as well as the rise of open architecture, stakeholders expect greater open access and sharing of data and information.

A *willingness to share* data and information on a project must exist. If people hoard data and information, the chances of having a useful PMIS will decline. Data is the "lifeblood" of a PMIS. If that blood does not flow into the repository, the PMIS will die from lack of use. Sharing by all stakeholders, within restrictions (for example, disclosing proprietary data to third parties), must occur. The days of hoarding data and information on projects as a power plan are vanishing. To hoard is to set oneself up as "not being a team player." A PMIS with open access rules enables people to share, rather than hide, data and information. In some cases, an argument can be made that the difficulty is not in the sharing of data and information, but in the exact opposite. With e-mail and distributed technology, the flood of data and information can be just paralyzing.

Stakeholders must treat data and the resulting information as very important resources on a project. If data is incomplete or tainted, information and decisions will be impacted, too. The typical attitude of just storing data for storage sake must disappear. Data and information must be given the same respect and attention as any other project resource: time, people, or equipment. In some respect, it can be argued that project managers need to place emphasis on data and information first because without it issues of time, people, and equipment cannot be dealt with effectively or efficiently. Data and information plays such an important role on a project that it requires the same delicate care as any other resource. Especially on technological and compliance projects, for example, data and information must be handled with extreme care because most decisions depend on their quality.

Building a useful PMIS requires understanding the context. Too often, project managers ignore the context of a project. They may, for instance, build what is referred to as an "administrative monolith" that retards rather than enhances project performance. Overemphasis on satisfying the needs of a PMIS component—for example, scheduling tool or generating reports—only makes decision making a challenge. The goal should be to adapt the PMIS to the context. More is not necessarily better when it comes to data and information. Too much of both can mean sensory overload, which can result in a failure to taking a PMIS seriously. Adding more technology may not be the answer, either. The key is scalability to contextual factors—for example, the geographical spread, the number of people, and cost.

Project managers should develop first a logical model of a PMIS and then a physical one. A logical model (Figure 2.2) addresses the needed functionalities to manage a project; it addresses *what* has to be done and not *how*. The physical models show how all the equipment, people, software, and data actually interact with each other to realize the logical model (Figure 2.3). Too often, project managers jump to the physical model, ignoring the logical one, creating a PMIS that fails to meet the needs of stakeholders and only adding to administrative overhead. A common example of placing the physical ahead of the logical model is when project managers purchase a tool, such as a scheduling software, before determining the desired functionalities and their relationships to each other. The result is often retrofitting the application to satisfy the requirements of the processes of the project or trying to adjust the processes to satisfy the tool. Either way, frustration and tension can arise.

Developing logical and physical models work best if the PMIS is viewed as a system whereby all the processes and components interact with one another according to

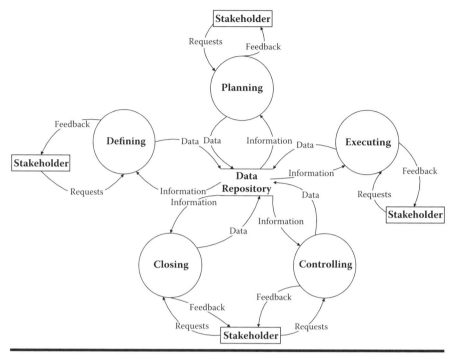

Figure 2.2   Logical model.

specific conditions or states. This systemic view is largely based upon the flow of data and its conversion to information. A systemic view not only allows understanding the flow of data under varying circumstances but also identifies any impact of changes to a PMIS. A project is a system that consists of objects, inputs, processes, and outputs. All four components must work together as smoothly as possible. Data is the one key element that enables these components to work together. Changing the quantity and quality of data can affect how these components work together to satisfy the goals and objects of a project.

Provide a supporting infrastructure for a PMIS. Any unsupported PMIS is a death signature. Lack of support is manifested in several ways. For instance, necessary tools, such as hardware and software, are not in the budget. Or management makes exceptions when providing data to the repository. Or, worse, management starts denigrating the contents, obviating its value to the project. As suggested in examples, management support plays an important role in ensuring that a PMIS plays an integral role. If key people view the PMIS as an administrative burden, its contributions to the overall performance of the project will be minimal, at best. The quality of the output of a PMIS is correlated with the quality of investment in its supporting infrastructure. Minimal investment has a high likelihood of providing poor results. Considerable time, effort, and other resources are required to develop, deploy, and

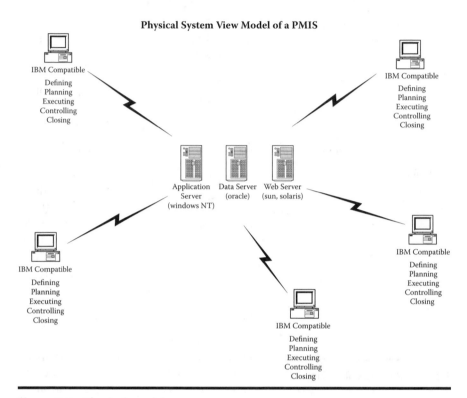

Physical System View Model of a PMIS

Figure 2.3   Physical model.

maintain a PMIS. Unfortunately, too often companies invest too little to cut costs, with the result of having a PMIS that costs much more in the long run.

Adopt a sunset approach toward data residing in a repository. Over time, a repository can collect a large quantity of data that rarely, if ever, is used to create information. Much of this data may be irrelevant because circumstances or requirements have changed. Keeping the data only creates problems, such as using greater information technology resources or tainting the quality of information. In addition, retaining "tainted" data can result in bad information which, in turn, influences decision making. A sunset approach can help to alleviate or eliminate these types of problems. As mentioned earlier, a repository can be populated with useless data. Data can become useless for many reasons— for example, time and relevancy to topic. For projects of long duration, it might help a project manager to purge or archive data from the repository to improve performance and increase the usefulness of the content.

Constantly monitor performance to ascertain process and product defects. Defects in process might be reflected in the cycle time for converting data into information and defect in product might be reflected in the degree of faulty information produced due to bad data. Statistics on process and product performance for a PMIS can help determine the quality of the contributions to performance. Of course, a project manager must develop, deploy, and maintain metrics on the overall performance of a PMIS to determine if a problem occurs and its impact. Metrics, however, should not be collected simply to show numbers. The key to a good metrics collection on any topic, and particularly on repository performance, is to collect data and generate information that improves the usefulness and performance of the repository. Too often measures are put in place that either tell no story or tell a story that no one cares about. Metrics for metrics' sake makes no sense because it wastes time and energy that could be better applied elsewhere on a project.

Identify essential, critical data. Not all data in a repository is equally pertinent. Some data is more valuable. Key stakeholders, as well as the goals and objectives of a project, will determine the degree of criticality. These criteria will help in determining the data to be purged from a repository, thereby reducing the opportunity for information overload and providing efficient operations. A project manager who understands the goals, objectives, and priorities of a project is likely to have the focus to avoid information flooding. Consequently, all data and information won't read as equally significant, which is rarely the case. By knowing what is of value in the repository, a project manager can distinguish between what to collect and process, as well as what to ignore or discard.

Promote sharing of data, limiting secrecy. If data is hoarded, a PMIS cannot provide a valuable service because the required data may not populate the repository. In other words, the repository is incomplete, and the information lacks reliability and validity. Incidentally, a lack of sharing of data reflects not only a lack of confidence in a PMIS, but also a lack of trust on a project. A good practice is to promote sharing of data, good or bad, by not deploying tactics like "shooting the messenger." On a project, the best practice is to restrict access to data and information only if it is absolutely necessary. If not, the best decision is to grant open access. Only in rare cases should data and information in a PMIS be restricted, and that is when the content is highly proprietary and secret from a governmental perspective.

Establish rules and standards for populating the repository. For example, create metadata, that is, data about data that will populate the repository. Apply controls like consistency requirements and range values for data. Anything noncompliant with such rules should raise a flag about data quality. The quality of the output—in this case, information—is based on the quality of the input or data. One of the best approaches for ensuring that the rules and standards are enforced is to designate someone on the project to serve as the single point of contact (SPOC). This person has the responsibility to collect data and information for the PMIS and then populate the content according to the rules and standards. The benefits are that the SPOC can ensure configuration management of the content and compliance with rules and standards.

Look for linkages among data. Often data is related in many ways; some obvious and others not so obvious. Linkage not only improves searching capabilities but also enables identifying opportunities to eliminate redundant data. It also removes the opportunity to create data "silos," which can result in overlooking key data and redundancy. It also allows taking a cross-functional perspective when data mining to determine relationships among data. Project managers might consider developing a good data model for their PMISs. This model helps to identify the logical relationships of the elements within the PMIS. If a DBMS is used, the combination of the data model and the metadata rules and standards should help to identify and manage the relationships among the data elements within a repository.

Take an ecological perspective of data, as suggested by Tom Davenport. Look at data as not some inert matter, but as an integral element of a dynamic environment that is affected by many forces that process data into information. Data cannot be divorced from the context of its environment. In the end, data and information are inseparable. For example, circumstances can change on a project. These include budget cuts, scope enlargement, schedule compression, and even mergers between two companies. Such circumstances will require revisiting a PMIS and will likely necessitate its redesign of data relationships, streamlining content through removal, or a combination of the two.

Fine Distinction

In the current version of the Project Management Body of Knowledge (PMBOK), the Project Management Institute (PMI) makes a distinction between a project management system (PMS) and a PMIS. According to the PMI, the former includes methodologies and procedures, whereas the latter, automated and integrated tools.

From the perspective of this book, a PMIS consists of both and makes no distinction. The reason is that systems can be either manual or automated, or a combination of both. Regardless, they must work together in an integrated and interdependent manner for a project to accomplish its goals objectively, efficiently, and effectively.

Never-Ending Construction

The reality is that constructing and maintaining a PMIS never ends. It requires constant attention of all stakeholders. The project manager, however, is the only person who is truly postured to ensure that an efficient but, more importantly, effective PMIS is in place.

A PMIS is only as good as its contents. If the data input lacks reliability and integrity, then the output will possess the same characteristics. It requires considerable attention by all stakeholders to ensure that the contents of a repository meet the highest standards possible for effective decision making.

Getting Started Checklist		
Question	*Yes*	*No*
1. Do you consider these components of your project management information system (PMIS)?		
Repository		
Technology		
Methodology		
Policies and procedures		
Stakeholders		
Forms		
Reports		
Principles, techniques, and tools of project management		
Environment (or context)		
2. Do you consider the components by considering these two characteristics?		
Integration		
Interdependence		
3. Do you determine any of the following principal activities?		
Retrieving data from different users		
Sending information to specific locations		
Transforming data and information		
Storing data and information		
Providing controls over the access and disbursal of data and information		
4. Have you identified all of the following potential challenges affecting the performance of a PMIS?		
Becoming a garbage bin collector of data		
Changing environmental conditions		
Slow performance		
5. Have you considered these consequences?		
Attention deficit		
Data bias		
Data correctness and incompleteness		
Data inconsistency		
Data irrelevance		
Data redundancy		
Data smog		

Getting Started Checklist (Continued)		
Question	*Yes*	*No*
Information overload		
Rush to judgment		
6. When looking at data, have you considered these three categories?		
Administrative		
Data values		
Data views		
7. Have you identified these roles?		
Data consumers		
Data custodians		
Data producers		
Information consumers		
Information manufacturers		
Information suppliers		
Product managers		
8. When developing, deploying, and maintaining a PMIS, do you consider these steps?		
Determine content		
Determine users		
Determine goals		
Determine hardware		
Determine software		
Provide supporting infrastructure		
Draft logical diagram		
Draft physical diagram		
Determine rules and standards for populating the repository		
Address considerations like scalability and portability		
Conduct a self audit of the data		
Deploy the PMIS		
Maintain and update the PMIS		
9. To keep the repository current, do you consider the following?		
Data cleansing		
Data mining		
Data replication		

Getting Started Checklist (Continued)		
Question	*Yes*	*No*
Data visualization and reporting of content		
10. Do you follow these key points to ensure that the PMIS successfully contributes to the outcome of a project?		
Adopt a sunset approach toward data residing in the repository.		
Allow access to data and information to the people needing it.		
Develop a logical model first and then a physical one.		
Encourage stakeholders to treat data and the resulting information as an important resource.		
Establish rules and standards for populating the repository.		
Identify essential, critical data.		
Instill a willingness to share data and information.		
Look for linkages among data.		
Perform constant monitoring of performance to ascertain process and product defects.		
Promote sharing of data and information by limiting secrecy.		
Provide a supporting infrastructure.		
Provide the right amount of data and information in the right format at the right level of detail		
Take an ecological perspective of data.		
Understand the context of the PMIS is employed.		
View the PMIS as a system whereby all the processes and components interact with one another according to specific conditions or states.		

Chapter 3

Personality Style and Communications

How project managers communicate with others on a project reflects their personality; how other stakeholders communicate also does the same. Their general approach reveals much about them by the information they value, the tools they choose, when and to whom they communicate, and why they communicate. In other words, communications reveals a person's preferences and, ultimately, their personality.

This point is illustrated to a large degree in what project managers deem important to populate a Project Management Information System (PMIS), what they use from it, and how they use the contents. Some project managers may select, for example, only summary information, whereas others may delve into the details. Yet others will rely less on content from the PMIS and more on what they hear from others. Nonetheless, a PMIS can provide an instrumental role in satisfying the particular personality needs of project managers when communicating.

Caveats

Several models are available to help project managers understand human behavior in general and communications preferences in particular. However, they should consider the following caveats.

First, all these models identify patterns of behavior, and not everyone fits into each category completely. It is risky, therefore, to force a person into a category within a model and attribute all the characteristics to that person. Project managers must observe a person over time and under varying circumstances to come to any reliable conclusion.

Second, these models are, like all models, mental constructs. They are an attempt to understand reality but are not reality and do not reflect it in its entirety. These models are incomplete and, therefore, should be considered tools for understanding human behavior.

Third, unlike physical science, behavioral science is inherently unpredictable. The behavioral aspects of a human being contain so many uncontrollable variables that, coupled with incompleteness in any model used and the knowledge about any person, make understanding human behavior as much an art as science.

Despite these caveats, the following can provide project managers with effective tools to look for patterns of behavior in general and communications in particular. Although not absolute, these models provide an effective approach to understanding one's own behavior, that of others, and the influence of both on one another. Project managers can interpret and respond in a manner that furthers project performance.

This chapter provides a sample of some popular models applied on projects used for understanding human behavior. There are, of course, so many more models of human behavior.

The Myers–Briggs Temperament

One of the most common models is the ever popular Myers–Briggs temperament types (Figure 3.1). The entire model is predicated upon four types of preferences. These types are, introversion versus extroversion; sensation versus intuition; thinking versus feeling; and perceiving versus judging. Choosing between each preference is a matter of degree; that is, a continuum between extremes exists.

Extroversion vs. Introversion	
• Obtains energy from outside themselves • Tends to be socially oriented	• Obtains energy from an internal source • Tends to be withdrawn
Sensate vs. Intuitive	
• Experiential-based • Tends towards practicality	• Looks towards the future • Favors hunches and possibilities
Thinking vs. Feeling	
• Emphasizes on logic • Stresses objectivity	• Values intimacy • Stresses relationships
Judging vs. Perceiving	
• Emphasizes finality • Is decisive	• Looks for options • Seeks complete information before making decisions

Figure 3.1 Myers–Briggs temperament summary table.

Extroversion (E) versus Introversion (I): Extroverts get their energy from outside themselves, often from other people in a social environment. Introverts get their energy from an internal source, such as being alone. The former are more socially oriented and feed off the external world; the latter tend towards being more withdrawn and feed off their internal orientation. An example of an extrovert is a project manager who places importance on engaging frequently with stakeholders. An example of an introvert is a project manager who engages with stakeholders infrequently and does so only when absolutely necessary.

Sensation (S) versus Intuition (N): Sensates people are those who are more experience-based. They tend toward practicality and what they perceive as occurring. In other words, they are realists. They focus on what is. Intuitive people look toward the future based on their hunches and possibilities. They are the dreamers or visionaries who focus on what could be. An example of a sensate is a project manager who stresses the importance of the here-and-now, such as current project performance. An example of an intuitive is a project manager who is less concerned with problems or issues as they currently exist, but could be more so later in the project.

Thinking (T) versus Feeling (F): Thinking people rely more on logic based upon the use of formal criteria and principles. They emphasize objectivity by considering the "head" over the "heart." Feeling people are subjective, valuing intimacy over distance, that is, the heart being more important than the head. An example of a thinking person is a project manager who emphasizes logical reasoning to derive a right solution to a problem. An example of a feeling person is a project manager who considers how a solution will impact the morale of the team and relationships with stakeholders.

Judging (J) versus Perceiving (P): Judging people emphasize finality. They are decisive, ensuring that closure to ambiguous situations comes quickly to meet a deadline. Perceiving people emphasize options and often appear hesitant to make decisions until they have more complete data and information. An example of a judging person is a project manager who makes decisions before all the facts and data have become available. An example of a perceiving person is a project manager who requires the complete facts and data to make a decision.

The combination of the four preferences creates four major temperaments: SP, SJ, NT, and NF (Figure 3.2).

SPs tend to be free, impulsive people who revel in the moment and have a proclivity toward action. An example is a project manager who acts quickly to address an issue with little or no analysis or consultation with others. SJs tend to be helpful and caretaking, who seek approval to further what should and ought to be done. An example is a project manager who consults with stakeholders, such as team members, before making a decision to act. NTs tend toward acquiring power

Preference	PM Style	Communications Style
SP	Probability towards action, e.g., minimal analysis	• Spontaneous communications • Open to different perspectives • Adaptable
SJ	Helpful and caretaking, e.g., consultative	• Formal, structured communications • Sees the world in black and white • Precise
NT	Power oriented and seeks mastery, e.g., assertive	• Emphasizes need for control or predictability • Seeks being objective, even impersonal
NF	Self-actualization, e.g., importance of goals	• Informal communications • Prefers qualitative over quantitative

Figure 3.2   Myers–Briggs temperament (preferences) summary table.

to dominate others and further their mastery, resulting in accomplishing their goals and those of organizations. An example is a project manager who is assertive in ensuring the accomplishment of project goals and objectives. NTs tend to be very task oriented. NFs tend toward self-actualization by maintaining integrity and meaning in whatever they do. An example is a project manager who stresses the importance of accomplishing the goals and objectives of a project through the talents, skills, and feelings of team members.

From these four major temperaments come sixteen patterns of behavior, or personalities. These are the INFP, ENFP, INFJ, ENFJ, ISFP, ESFP, ISFJ, ESFJ, INTP, ENTP, INTJ, ENTJ, ISTP, ISTJ, ESTP, and ESTJ.

Each of the four major temperaments has its own proclivities on how it communicates with others.

As communicators, SPs are spontaneous in their communications, open to different perspectives, and adaptable based upon what they hear from others. An example is a project manager who seeks the advice and counsel of many stakeholders through an informal approach. SJs prefer a more formal, structured approach when communicating, and do so in a manner that conveys ideas in black and white rather than in grays; whatever they communicate will be precise and leave little opportunity for interpretation. An example is a project manager who relies on formal communications with stakeholders, such as regularly scheduled meetings. NTs communicate in a way that is based upon criteria or principles, and will emphasize their need for control and predictability; they will also take a formal approach toward communications in an effort to appear objective, even impersonal. An example is a project manager who interacts infrequently with stakeholders and does so sparingly. NTs' reports are often sparse in content and to the point. NFs communicate informally and emphasize qualitative rather than quantitative factors, such as values. NTs will emphasize understanding and looking at possibilities or

Behavioral Style	Characteristics	Communication Style
Expediter	• Task oriented and assertive	• Communicate to, not with, people
Communicator	• People oriented and assertive	• Communicate with, not to, people
Administrator	• Task oriented and low key	• Communicate formally and only when must
Planner	• People oriented and low key	• Communicate on personal level and spontaneously

Figure 3.3   Birkman model summary table.

options. An example is a project manager who interacts informally with stakeholders to gauge feelings about the performance of a project.

The Birkman Model

This model uses color to identify types of behavioral, or preferred, styles. The four colors make up a grid. These preferred styles reflect one's perceptions, e.g., mental images and assumptions (that is, response based upon perceptions, and socialized behavior and actions). Like the Myers–Briggs model, most people show one pattern of behavior.

The Birkman model is created by the intersection of two continuums, low key versus assertive, and task-oriented versus people-oriented (Figure 3.3).

The task-oriented and assertive types are called *expediters* and are represented by the color red. These people are frank and to the point. They emphasize action over discussion. There is very little "fluff" in regard to thought or action. An example is a project manager who spends very little time and effort collecting facts and data or examining logical conclusions before taking action.

The people-oriented and assertive types are called *communicators* and are represented by the color green. These people are very competitive in a positive way and embrace new ideas. They are quite flexible in thought and action when dealing with other people. An example is a project manager who prefers to explore options before taking action. The task-oriented and low-key types are called *administrators* and are represented by the color yellow. These people are very orderly and cautious in thought and action. They prefer routine and structure and are reluctant to step "outside the box." An example is a project manager who prefers to establish the supporting infrastructure before the actual execution of a project.

The people-oriented and low-key types are the *planners* and are represented by the color blue. These people are very reflective in thought and provide insights that are often creative. They prefer intimacy when working with people. An example is a project manager who prefers to develop a detailed schedule before the actual execution of a project.

Each of the four behavioral styles has its own proclivities on how it communicates with others.

Expediters will communicate *to* people and not *with* people. Being competitive and assertive, they are more oriented towards formality and directness in their communications. An example is a project manager who gives direction on what to do on a project, either formally or informally. Communicators will communicate *with* people and not *to* people. They will concentrate on influencing rather than telling people because they are often friendly and approachable. They use good listening skills. An example is a project manager who concentrates on developing interpersonal relationships with stakeholders to gain an understanding of an issue before taking action. Administrators will take the formal route to communications and will communicate only if put in a situation to do so. Because they are on their guard, they will communicate on an impersonal level. An example is a project manager who relies on formal approaches for communicating at regular intervals. Planners will communicate on a personable level and do so spontaneously. They are likely to exercise good listening skills. An example is a project manager who develops a plan with the participation and feedback of different stakeholders.

Color Code

Another color model, although less known, is the one developed by Taylor Hartman. This model uses color to represent one of four personalities. Personality, according to Hartman, reflects the traits as well as strengths and weaknesses of people in how they think, feel, and act. All behavior becomes motivated by satisfying the needs and wants of a specific personality.

The four personalities are reflected in the four colors: red, blue, white, and yellow (Figure 3.4).

The *Red Personalities*, called "power wielders," are motivated by acquiring power. They have a strong desire to maintain control. They emphasize action and production and, not surprisingly, are assertive and competitive. An example is a project manager who takes control of a project and pursues immediate action.

The *Blue Personalities*, called "do gooders," are motivated by intimacy and accomplish that through reflection and empathy. They emphasize the importance

Personality	Characteristics	Communications Style
Red	• Seeks power • Desires to maintain control	• Direct • Logically oriented
Blue	• Seeks intimacy • Is reflective	• Informal • Empathetic
White	• Seeks peace • Avoids confrontation	• Formal • Indirect
Yellow	• Seeks excitement • Seeks attention, action, and praise	• Informal • Spontaneous • Expressive

Figure 3.4   Color code summary table.

of the heart over the head, thereby placing importance on emotion. An example is a project manager who emphasizes the need to build esprit de corps.

The *White Personalities,* called "peace keepers," are motivated through peace. They attempt to avoid confrontation by preferring diplomatic approaches, thereby restraining their feelings toward individuals or issues. They are often the silent ones. An example is a project manager who avoids conflict to encourage people to get along.

The *Yellow Personalities,* called "fun lovers," are motivated by excitement. They want attention, action, and praise. They want to have fun in whatever they do and, therefore, are playful and lively. An example is a project manager who likes to consider options, even experiment, to solve problems.

Each of the four personalities has its own proclivities on how it communicates with others.

Red personalities will be direct in their communications with an emphasis on getting to the point. They are also likely to place little emphasis on the emotions surrounding a discussion, or fluff, and more on logic. They will communicate to and not with people. An example is a project manager who rarely strays from the main point of a discussion, and when he or she does, does so formally. Blue personalities will communicate informally and intimately. They emphasize the subjective nature of communications and are good listeners because of their strong empathic skills. An example is a project manager who uses interpersonal skills to communicate. White personalities are more formal and indirect in their communications to avoid confrontation. However, their good listening skills enable them to develop compromises that lessen the opportunity for discord; their emotions are masked from others. An example is a project manager who often communicates directly on an issue. Yellow personalities take an informal, spontaneous approach toward communicating. Being expressive, they are less likely to listen effectively because they prefer to talk. An example is a project manager who uses a considerable number of positive verbiage in a casual environment to encourage action.

Multiple Intelligences

People often assume that only one intelligence exists, which is defined as the ability to learn and respond to circumstances, past and present. Often, this intelligence is in the form of verbal and logical thinking. However, Howard Gardener has pioneered the concept of multiple intelligences and has identified seven of them. He says that each intelligence has unique cognitive processes that determine how one learns and responds to circumstances. These seven intelligences are linguistic, spatial, musical, bodily-kinesthetic, logical–mathematical, interpersonal, and intrapersonal (Figure 3.5).

Linguistic intelligence is exercised through words and often involves activities such as arguing and instructing. *Spatial intelligence* is exercised through images and

Intelligence	Characteristics	Communications Style
Linguistic	• Argumentative and instructive	• Emphasizes use of words to communicate ideas and thoughts
Spatial	• Image oriented, creative, and transformative	• Emphasizes images and other visual systems
Musical	• Sound oriented and produces melodies	• Communicates with sounds and identify patterns in ideas and data
Bodily-Kinesthetic	• Physical actions and body movement	• Uses body language and objects
Logical-Mathematical	• Logical, using reasoning and sequencing	• Is formal, emphasizing numbers and sequence
Interpersonal	• People oriented, working with and motivating other people	• Either formally or informally, with stress on encouraging interaction
Intrapersonal	• Understanding of one's self, involving self-reflection	• Using empathy by attunement to one's feelings

Figure 3.5   Multiple intelligence summary table.

involves activities such as creating and transforming. *Musical intelligence* is exercised through sounds and involves activities such as producing melodies. *Bodily-kinesthetic intelligence* is exercised through physical actions and involves activities such as body movement. *Logical–mathematical intelligence* is exercised through logic and involves activities such as using numbers, which requires reasoning and sequencing. *Interpersonal intelligence* is exercised through dealing with other people and involves activities such as working with and motivating other people. *Intrapersonal intelligence* is exercised through understanding one's self, mainly psychological, and involves activities such as self-reflection.

People dominated by any one of the intelligences just described have their own proclivities on how they communicate with others.

People with linguistic intelligence will emphasize the use of words to communicate ideas and thoughts, and do so persuasively and instructively. For example, a project manager may emphasize narrative reports over charts populated with metrics. People with spatial intelligence will use images and other visualizations to communicate with other people. For example, a project manger may prefer pictures to communicate a point over using narrative text. People with musical intelligence will communicate with sound (which has minimum applicability in a project environment); however, they tend to identify and communicate patterns reflected in ideas and data. For example, a project manager may pinpoint patterns of behavior rolled from details rather than focus on a single detail as being important. People with bodily-kinesthetic intelligence will communicate with their body (which, again, is rare in the project environment); however, they can demonstrate ideas and information by using their bodies and objects during presentations. For example, a project manager may prefer to communicate in front of an audience, such as a steering committee, using a slide show. People with logical–mathematical intelligence will formally communicate ideas and information, emphasizing numbers and sequence. For example, a project manager may prefer to concentrate on quantifiable results, such as the Schedule Performance Index (SPI) or Cost Performance Index (CPI). People with interpersonal skills will likely communicate either formally or informally, but in a way that encourages good interaction using skills related to speaking and listening. For example, a project manager may prefer to meet one-on-one with stakeholders to understand a problem and develop a solution. People with intrapersonal skills will likely communicate in a way that demonstrates either control or lack of control over their feelings and be able to use their own perspective as a basis to understand others. For example, a project manager may seek isolation from others to contemplate a solution to a problem and then communicate the decision.

Enneagram

The Enneagram has been around for awhile. Based upon Sufi teaching, it identifies nine personality types that reflect patterns of behavior through unique thoughts and feelings. By understanding these patterns a person can see the world through different points of view under normal and stressful situations (Figure 3.6).

The relationships between these nine personality types are based upon an arrangement of lines that intersect to form nine points within a circle. Each point

Personality Type	Characteristics	Communications Style
Perfectionist	• Prescriptive and normative focus	• Formal, coupled with logic
Giver	• Pursues approval and affection of others	• Informal, coupled with empathy
Performer	• Competitive and achievement oriented	• Informal, with preference for action
Tragic Romantic	• Dominated by emotions and seeks authenticity	• Informal, emphasizing emotions
Observer	• Objective and independent	• Formal, with detachment
Devil's Advocate	• Identifies with underdog and clashes with authority	• Informal, with empathy
Epicure	• Dilettantism and options oriented	• Informal, spontaneous
Boss	• Power seeker over people and situations	• Formal, emphasizing goal attainment
Mediator	• Agreement and consensus oriented, dealing with situation indirectly	• Formal, with ability to see multiple perspectives

Figure 3.6 Enneagram summary table.

represents a personality type and is grouped into triads: feeling, doing, and relating. Each point is identified by a number, from 1 through 9.

Using the work of Helen Palmer in *The Enneagram: Understanding Yourself and the Others in Your Life,* this author will use her names to describe each personality:

Perfectionists (Point 1) are people who have a prescriptive and normative focus. They are often critical thinkers. They have very little room for trial and error. Rather, they focus on doing what is perceived as correct or right. They have little tolerance for ambiguity. For example, a project manager may not make a decision until all facts and data are available.

Givers (Point 2) are pursuers of approval and the affection of others. They want to be liked and accepted by people who are in authoritative positions and among equals. They are outwardly focused to the point that they may lose their identity as individuals to satisfy others. They seek to be caregivers but not without the potential for reward from the ones they seek affection and approval. For example, a project manager may seek the advice and counsel from everyone on the team before making a decision.

Performers (Point 3) are the competitors and achievers. They seek external rewards based upon action matter than thought. They seek achievement to attain status and respect. Not surprisingly, they are extremely focused. For example, a project manager prefers to use external, rather than internal, incentives to achieve the goals of a project.

Tragic Romantics (Point 4) are idealistic. They are dominated by emotions, or the heart. As they are highly self-critical, these people are somewhat negative and often become "outsiders" in a group. They strive for authenticity and will pursue it at the expense of alienating others. For example, a project manager emphasizes the "people side" over the "task side" of project management.

Observers (Point 5) want their space from others. They prefer objectivity and independence rather than becoming wrapped up in the emotions of others or of a given circumstance. They prefer to collect the facts and data first and then draw objective conclusions about what they observed. For example, a project manager emphasizes logic, data, and information over values.

Devil's Advocates (Point 6) identify with the underdog and, therefore, often clash with authority. They are often suspicious of the motives and behavior of others in authority. They draw battle lines in their support of the underdog, resulting in a "we versus they" approach toward dealing with circumstances. For example, a project manager may often side with the team rather than the end user when issues arise.

Epicures (Point 7) are the "jack of all trades and the master of none." They are dilettantes who seek adventure over routine, and pleasure over pain. To avoid being trapped, they continuously keep their options open as they pursue the positive side of life. Emphasizing multiple experiences, they are able to provide creative insights on solving problems and dealing with difficult circumstances. For example, a project manager prefers to deal with the "big picture" issues rather than delve into the details, preferring to give direction over doing.

Bosses (Point 8) are protectors and take charge. They are motivated by power and control over others and situations. Their style emphasizes less deliberation and more action. They are often assertive and can become aggressive when placed in confrontational situations. For example, a project manager may prefer making a decision alone rather than seeking the advice and counsel of others.

Mediators (Point 9) seek agreement with other people; failure to achieve that agreement creates internal turmoil. Often they are indirect when dealing with negative issues to avoid confrontation. They prefer order and predictability over anything ambiguous because both bring comfort when relating to others. They have the ability to see multiple points of view and, consequently, seek solutions to problems or issues that satisfy most or all of the parties. For example, a project manager may seek compromises over confrontation or competition to solve a problem or deal with an issue.

People dominated by one of the patterns just described have their own proclivities on how they communicate with others.

Perfectionists have a formal communications style that emphasizes quantification and logic to support their points. They have little desire to listen because they already know the correct answer or the truth. For example, a project manager may use hard logic as the primary means to support his or her points. Givers use an informal approach when communicating and remain attuned to the emotional relationships with listeners as well as being emphatic at the same time. For example, a project manager may rely on interpersonal skills, such as one-on-one sessions, to communicate with stakeholders. Performers are also informal communicators because they emphasize action rather than lengthy communications to achieve results quickly; they listen to get what they need. For example, a project manager may rely on cursory information and quickly act. Tragic romantics are informal communicators who emphasize our emotion over logic and communicate qualitatively at a high level; they are good listeners but sometimes their emotions interfere with their listening. For example, a project manager will talk more about the vision of a project rather than discuss the details. Observers communicate formally, preferring logic and detachment with whom they communicate; however, they employ good listening skills. For example, a project manager may rely on facts, data, and logic to communicate with stakeholders. Devil's advocates use an informal approach when communicating, and they communicate with great emotion and at a qualitative level. Being highly skeptical, they do not place much importance on listening effectively. For example, a project manager may require substantial time and effort to convince him or her to change the direction of a project. Epicures are informal communicators who do so spontaneously and at a high level. Because they are very expressive, they lack the patience to listen effectively. For example, a project manager may talk more and listen less to encourage enthusiasm about completing a project successfully. Bosses prefer formal communications and do so based upon their logic. They lack the necessary tolerance to listen effectively because their focus is on furthering their own goals. For example, a project manager may apply selective hearing to substantiate his or her thoughts about a problem or issue. Mediators use formal communications because it is often an effective means to avoid confrontation by providing the necessary distance from people. However, they can be effective listeners if they use their ability to see multiple points of view and then derive a solution that will satisfy most or all people. For example, a project manager may seek to understand all viewpoints prior to communicating a significant decision.

Herrmann Brain Dominance

Next to Myers–Briggs, the Herrmann Brain Dominance typology is frequently used to understand human behavior in general and communications in particular. This model presents a quadrant-based model of the human brain; each quadrant is called a preference. It is predicated on the assumption that the brain can be grouped into four processing models and that most people reflect one of these preferences: *Analyzer* (A quadrant); *Organizer* (B quadrant); *Personalizer* (C quadrant); and *Visualizer* (D quadrant) (Figure 3.7).

Analyzers are very logical and analytical. They stress the importance of facts and data and take a quantitative perspective. They tolerate very little "fluff," preferring precision and clarity over ambiguity, and analysis over synthesis. For example, a project manager relies more on metrics to assess a project's status than the assessment by key team members.

Organizers prefer structure and organization to minimize any ambiguity and confusion. They develop or adopt plans and methodologies as a way to reduce confusion and ambiguity. They place importance on control by focusing on the vision using structure and order. They seek stability. For example, a project manager establishes a wide array of formal disciplines on a project prior to its execution.

Personalizers are humanists. They like to interact with people and are expressive. They make good team members and build teams by addressing and resolving interpersonal conflicts that frequently arise in groups. Personalizers have a keen insight into their own emotions and those of others. For example, a project manager uses

Preference	Characteristics	Communications Style
Analyzer	• Is logical and analytical	• Formal and unemotional, stressing quantification
Organizer	• Prefers structure and organization	• Formal, presenting points in a structured format and buttressed with detail
Personalizer	• Likes to interact with people	• Informal, interpersonal, using good listening skills
Visualizer	• Concentrates on the big picture, synthesizing different ideas	• Informal, communicating visually with metaphors and diagrams

Figure 3.7   Herrmann Brain Dominance summary table.

his or her interpersonal skills to determine the cause of a problem rather than wade through piles of data to find the answer.

Visualizers are the visionaries and "big picture" people. They like to investigate and synthesize different ideas in a way that often results in unique, creative visions. They are also risk takers, having a willingness to experiment to see if the vision can become a reality. They are able to not just develop the vision but also have the ability to motivate others to partake in its realization. Visualizers also rely more on intuition than facts and data when creating a vision. For example, a project manager prefers to focus on the vision and overall schedule performance rather than the details of a project plan.

People dominated by any one of the preferences described in the preceding text have their own proclivities on how they communicate with others.

Analyzers are people who emphasize facts and data and place great importance on independence and objectivity. Their communications is formal and quite unemotional, stressing logic and quantification. For example, a project manager prefers formal rather than informal meetings with stakeholders. Organizers communicate formally, too, but present their points in a structured format that is buttressed with detailed information. They emphasize the need for consistency in communications. For example, a project manager prefers a presentation packed with metrics when presenting the status of a project. However, personalizers prefer doing so interpersonally. They will place importance on emotional issues and emphasize the need to relate to listeners. They will apply good listening skills to ensure sharing information and persuasion. For example, a project manager prefers informal working sessions to talk with other team members to share information and obtain feedback. Visualizers communicate the big picture and discuss the importance of how everything should fit together. They communicate visually and use metaphors and diagrams. They focus on the reasons behind a vision and less on the details supporting it. For example, a project manager prefers to talk about the overall view of a project, for example, systems perspective, rather than delve into the details.

Organizational Engineering

Although it is a sociological model empathizing complementary skills and compatibility among team members of a group, Organizational Engineering (OE) provides an effective insight into how people approach work situations, especially when communicating. OE identifies four styles: *Reactive Stimulator* (RS), *Logical Processor* (LP), *Hypothetical Analyzer* (HA), and *Relational Innovator* (RI). These four styles are derived from a matrix that is formed by the intersection of two continuums: method and mode. Method is the preferred approach for decision making, which is structured or unpatterned. Mode is the preferred response, which is thought or action (Figure 3.8).

Style	*Characteristics*	*Communications Style*
Reactive Stimulator	• Desires to act immediately • Values independence	• Informal and direct
Logical Processor	• Is logical and methodical • Seeks detail and precision	• Formal, with concentration on a narrow topic, impatient listener
Hypothetical Analyzer	• Seeks options before acting • Is analytical and definitive	• Formal, with excellent listening skills
Relational Innovator	• Likes to explore each option • Is theoretical and innovative	• Informal and communicates at a summary, abstract level

Figure 3.8   Organizational engineering summary table.

Reactive stimulators move quickly; that is, they want to act right away. They want immediate satisfaction from their actions. They value independence and therefore want minimal supervision, rules, or structure. Change is embraced because the status quo is too constrictive. For example, a project manager prefers to act, rather than collect all the facts and data first.

Logical processors are logical and methodical. They value predictability and order. Detail and precision are key to performing a task "right." They do not like to operate in a cloud of ambiguity, and, therefore, like to pursue concrete goals using specific, detailed instructions. However, they do not like close supervision because they value self-reliance. For example, a project manager prefers to have all the facts and data before taking any action.

Hypothetical analyzers develop options before acting. They are highly analytical and definitive in their pursuit. They are especially adept at solving problems, being careful to distinguish causes from symptoms. Hypothetical analyzers like to see the big picture by identifying the major components of a system, for example, and their relationships among each one. They have a tolerance for structure and methodology when addressing an issue or problem. For example, a project manager prefers to have the infrastructure (e.g., communications plan) in place prior to acting.

Relational innovators define and redefine goals. They like challenges that provide the opportunity to develop options and explore each one. They are highly theoretical and innovative. Relational innovators are nonlinear thinkers who have no problem straying off on a tangent and coming up with outside-the box-solutions to problems or issues. They are abstract thinkers. For example, a project manager prefers to focus on the vision of a project and see how everything fits together to determine the preferred approach.

People dominated by any one of the primary styles described previously have their own proclivities on how they communicate with others.

Reactive stimulators place great emphasis on action and, therefore, rely more on informal communication and getting to the point. They communicate at a higher level and listen only enough to get the job done. They communicate at a summary level. For example, a project manager prefers to informally go to the appropriate person to obtain the information he or she needs rather than consult a team. Relational innovators also rely on information communications and do so at a summary level. However, they will take more time to understand the total picture because they are people oriented. For example, a project manager prefers talking about data at a summary level rather than in any particular detail. Logical processors communicate formally. Their focus is on acquiring detail in a narrow area. Being very production oriented, they do not take much time listening to people; they only do so to get the detail information that they need. For example, a project manager prefers to delve into the details of a narrow subject area rather than discuss the project at a higher level. Hypothetical analyzers rely upon formal communications to meet their information needs. They tend to be good listeners because they are people oriented and are willing to take the time to get the data and information they need. For example, a project manager prefers to meet in a formal setting (e.g., regularly scheduled meetings) to hold discussions or share information.

Many Models

The models described above are, of course, just a subset of a much bigger population of them. The key is for project managers to select a model that can help them communicate effectively on a project, both from their own perspective and from that of others. Because projects managers spend more than 90 percent of their time communicating, and the results of their projects reflect how well team members interact, they should be aware of the models available to them. Of course, project managers need to recognize that these models are not like the mechanical calculation of the critical path. Rather, they are more like heuristics because too many uncontrollable and unknowable variables exist that affect human behavior.

Getting Started Checklist		
Question	Yes	No
1. If you decide to apply the Myers-Briggs Temperament Model, do you understand the difference between:		
Extroversion versus Introversion?		
Sensation versus Intuition?		
Thinking versus Feeling?		
Judging versus Perceiving?		
The communications styles of each personality, e.g., ISTJ, ENFP?		
2. If you decide to apply the Birkman Model, do you understand the characteristics of:		
Administrators?		
Communicators?		
Expeditors?		
Planners?		
The communications style of each one?		
3. If you decide to apply the Color Code, do you understand the characteristics of:		
Blue personalities?		
Red personalities?		
White personalities?		
Yellow Personalities?		
The communications style of each one?		
4. If you decide to apply the concept of Multiple Intelligences, do you understand the characteristics of:		
Bodily-kinesthetic intelligence?		
Interpersonal intelligence?		
Intrapersonal intelligence?		
Linguistic intelligence?		
Logical–mathematical intelligence?		
Musical intelligence?		
Spatial intelligence?		
The communications style of each one?		

Getting Started Checklist (Continued)		*Yes*	*No*
5.	If you decide to apply the Enneagram, do you understand the characteristics of:		
	Bosses?		
	Devil's Advocates?		
	Epicures?		
	Givers?		
	Mediators?		
	Observers?		
	Perfectionists?		
	Performers?		
	Tragic Romantics?		
	The communications style of each one?		
6.	If you decide to apply the Herrmann Brain Dominance Model, do you understand the characteristics of:		
	Analyzers?		
	Organizers?		
	Personalizers?		
	Visualizers?		
	The communications style of each one?		
7.	If you decide to apply the Organizational Engineering Model, do you understand the characteristics of:		
	Hypothetical analyzers?		
	Logical processors?		
	Reactive stimulators?		
	Relational innovators?		
	The communications style of each one?		■

Chapter 4

Applying Active and Effective Listening

Listening is an attribute that, everyone agrees, is important, yet few people, including project managers, actually practice it. The following saying summarizes the importance of listening: "God gave so much importance to listening over talking that He gave people two ears and only one mouth."

Project Management Information System (PMIS) Contributions

A PMIS can make significant contributions to active and effective listening. One major contribution is that it provides data and information for corroboration of what project managers hear and listen from others; the perception of others may differ from what the content in a PMIS reveals. Another major contribution is that it provides background material for asking questions when listening.

Active and Effective Listening

Two closely related sets of listening skills exist: active and effective.

Active listening occurs when the listener attempts to understand as clearly as possible what the speaker says. Effective listening is attempting to understand the perspective of the speaker and empathize, not sympathize, with him or her.

Project managers must exercise both skills because they have to interact and communicate with many stakeholders. Both skills enable project managers to understand the interests of each stakeholder and how to align those interests to achieve the goals and objectives of their projects.

Two Important Reasons

The reality is that project managers must be active and effective listeners simultaneously for two very important reasons.

First, they deal with many issues. They are the only "linchpin" on a project and must deal with multidisciplinary issues and problems. Being a linchpin requires involvement with people from many different fields and getting them, on many occasions, to work together to solve problems and achieve the goals of a project. Active and effective listening enables project managers to understand the perspectives and needs of these disciplines.

Second, they deal with many stakeholders with varying backgrounds. Each stakeholder has a different interest in the outcome of a project and views it from his or her own perspective. This circumstance allows conflict to occur any time during the project life cycle. If a project manager fails to listen actively and effectively, he or she may face conflict, producing negative effects.

For purposes set forth here, active and effective listening are combined and subsumed under listening. Combining both makes good sense for one reason: a project manager really cannot divorce one from the other. To effectively listen, he or she must listen actively. To listen actively, he or she must listen effectively. Although both are distinct conceptually in their implementation it is virtually impossible to separate one from the other.

For example, project managers frequently have to find the source of a problem or issue. Often, the source is not obvious. It requires asking questions and clarifying what is said to understand the cause. People frequently see circumstances and even causes from different vantage points. By combining active and effective listening, project managers can gain a good understanding of the real cause behind a problem.

Why Few People Listen Effectively

Listening sometimes does not come easy. Often, the difficulty is not because people are not willing to listen but because they are unable to do so. Their mind does not allow them to see the total picture because they are only able to see the world in one dimension. This inability to listen using both sides of the brain can cause miscommunication, misinterpretation, and miscalculation. The result can be a listener who is unable to deal with not only the logic of a relationship but with the emotional component either. Hence, this asymmetrical use of the brain often results in the inability of the listener to absorb all the necessary cues from the person speaking.

Effective and active listening requires, therefore, using both sides of the brain. Unfortunately, few people understand this fact. Instead, they see this skill as one reflecting the use of the right or left side of the brain.

The left side of the brain emphasizes facts, logical thinking and reasoning, organization, and discipline and precision in thought. It is highly goal and analysis oriented. Effective and active listening solely from this perspective can result in overlooking the importance of the emotional message of the speaker; for example, the emphasis on calculating metrics is a left-brain activity. Focusing on schedule and cost performance indices as a measure of success is a prime example of left-brain thinking.

The right side of the brain emphasizes emotions and sensory perception. Imaging and imagining are two salient activities of this side of the brain. The emphasis is on nonverbal communications and spontaneous behavior. Effective and active listening from this perspective can result in ignoring important facts and data, and being influenced by the speaker. The emphasis on teaming, esprit de corps, and creativity are three examples of right-brain thinking. Less emphasis is on facts, data, and logic, and more on the people side of project management.

Taking a holistic approach towards listening requires considerable discipline on the part of the listener. The reason is that listeners tend to fall into their comfort zones by absorbing what they *want* to hear and ignoring what they *need* to hear. This screening can result in selective hearing that can lead to incorrect conclusions based upon inconclusive data and information. Listening is as much art as science, and the opportunity for error is large. By not using both sides of the brain, the likelihood of error increases dramatically.

Four Steps for Effective and Active Listening

To listen well using both sides of the brain, project managers should perform these actions: hear, clarify, interpret, and respond (Figure 4.1).

Hear

To listen actively and effectively, a project manager must be a good hearer. Hearing involves picking up the sounds of the speaker by performing these actions:

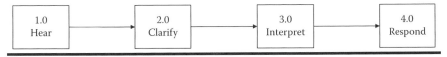

Figure 4.1   Listening flowchart.

- Allow the other person to talk, not just the project manager.
- Avoid interruptions, unless it is absolutely necessary.
- Clear one's mind of distractions, e.g., other priorities.
- Clear the environment of distractions, e.g., noise.
- Encourage the speaker to expound on what is being said through verbal and nonverbal cues on the part of the project manager.
- Focus on the speaker, e.g., maintain eye contact.
- Listen to what is said and not how it is said.
- Model the speaker's physical behavior to encourage further talking.
- Observe nonverbal behavior as well as what is said.
- Recognize that hearing is a psychological and physiological process.
- Recognize the influence of verbal and nonverbal behavior.
- Strive to eliminate any preconceived notions, e.g., stereotypes and prejudgments.
- Use open-ended questions to encourage the speaker to continue talking.

A common example of violating the above actions is a project manager who feels that he or she has to do all the talking. Not only that, he or she ignores comments that are contrary, resulting in selective hearing. The statement "tell me what I want to hear and not what I need to hear" summarizes this action.

Clarify

Upon hearing the speaker, the next step for a project manager is to clarify what was said. Often, what is said is not completely or accurately heard. Although the speaker has the responsibility to ensure that what he or she said is understood, the reality is that the listener must make some effort, too, and the onus rests with the latter. Here are some steps to help clarify what was said:

- Acknowledge the feelings behind what is said.
- Ask questions to probe for further detail.
- Avoid asking leading questions to get the desired comment or response.
- Avoid coming to conclusions before the speaker finishes.
- Be cognizant of the speaker's choice and application of words .
- Encourage feedback through questioning.
- Follow up on clichés and platitudes.
- Keep all of your questions pertinent to the topic.
- Look for indicators of selective perception either on the project manager's part or the speaker's.
- Look for synchronicity between what was said and body language.
- Maintain two-way communication.
- Paraphrase what was said and verify for accuracy.

- Think critically about what was said but don't display critical behavior.
- Try to separate assumptions from facts and data.

The biggest challenge facing project managers when seeking clarification is the failure to ask questions that probe to determine the cause of a problem or situation. Instead, they either think they must develop a solution right away or they already know the answer. Questions, to them, are either asked perfunctorily or seen as a waste of time.

Interpret

After clarifying what the speaker said, be ready to interpret the message. Interpretation requires ascertaining not only the credibility behind what the speaker said but also an understanding of what was said. Here are some steps for interpreting a speaker's remarks:

- Avoid taking what the speaker says at face value by looking at feelings as well as body language.
- Communicate your interpretation and verify its accuracy.
- Concentrate on facts and data, not perceptions.
- Distinguish between assumptions, and facts and data.
- Identify the main ideas.
- Pay attention to nonverbal communications to determine sincerity about what is said.
- Recognize the influence of one's thoughts and perceptions on the topic.

The halo effect can prove the biggest challenge to interpreting what is said. Project managers, like all other humans, can find their interpretations as being the result of a characteristic of the person speaking. They can end up exercising selective hearing that can ultimately result in erroneous thinking and coming to inaccurate conclusions.

Respond

Finally, the project manager will likely have to respond to what the speaker said. Of the four steps, this one is optional. Any response will have a physiological, emotional, and psychological aspect to it. Here are some steps to respond effectively:

- Be sincere in offering help.
- Conduct follow-up, if necessary, on any resulting request by the project manager or the speaker.

- Demonstrate a physiological (e.g., body language) and psychological response.
- Exhibit empathy rather than sympathy.
- Exhibit verbal and nonverbal cues that build bridges rather than walls between the project manager and the speaker.
- Seek feedback on your response.

An example of good response is that a project manager might set a time to revisit an issue or problem to discuss the effectiveness of any solution to it. Such action is absolutely critical to ensure that any recommendations or solutions to the issue or problem have been dealt with effectively.

The Most Important Skill

Listening is the hardest communications skill. So many circumstances require it; so few project managers practice it. Of course, they are not alone in this regard. Yet, project managers need to be premier listeners because they must deal with a wide range and number of stakeholders. If they fail to listen, project managers cannot reasonably expect a stakeholder to become partially or fully engaged on a project.

Getting Started Checklist			
Question		*Yes*	*No*
1.	Are you regularly applying active listening?		
2.	Are you regularly applying effective listening?		
3.	When you hear, do you:		
	Allow the other person to talk, not just the project manager?		
	Avoid interruptions, unless it is absolutely necessary?		
	Clear the environment of distractions, e.g., noise?		
	Encourage the speaker to expound on what is said through verbal and nonverbal cues on the part of the project manager?		
	Focus on the speaker, e.g., maintain eye contact?		
	Listen to what is said and not how it is said?		
	Model the speaker's physical behavior to encourage further talking?		
	Observe nonverbal behavior as well as what is said?		

Getting Started Checklist (Continued)		
Question	Yes	No
Recognize that hearing is a psychological and physiological process?		
Recognize the influence of verbal and nonverbal behavior?		
Strive to eliminate any preconceived notions, e.g., stereotypes, prejudgments?		
Use open-ended questions to encourage the speaker to continue talking?		
4. When you clarify, do you:		
Acknowledge the feelings behind what is said?		
Ask questions to probe for further detail?		
Avoid asking leading questions to get the desired comment or response?		
Avoid coming to conclusions before the speaker finishes?		
Be cognizant of the speaker's choice and application of words?		
Encourage feedback through questioning?		
Follow up on clichés and platitudes?		
Keep all of your questions pertinent to the topic?		
Look for indicators of selective perception either on the project manager's part or the speaker's?		
Look for synchronicity between what was said and body language?		
Maintain two-way communication?		
Paraphrase what was said and verify for accuracy?		
Think critically about what was said but don't display critical behavior?		
Try to separate assumptions from facts and data?		
5. When you interpret, do you:		
Avoid taking what the speaker says at face value by looking at feelings as well as body language?		
Communicate your interpretation and verify its accuracy?		
Concentrate on facts and data, not perceptions?		
Distinguish between assumptions and facts and data?		
Identify the main ideas?		
Pay attention to nonverbal communications to determine sincerity about what is said?		

Getting Started Checklist (Continued)		
Question	*Yes*	*No*
Recognize the influence of one's thoughts and perceptions on the topic?		
6. When you respond, do you:		
Be sincere in offering help?		
Conduct follow-up, if necessary, on any resulting request by the project manager or the speaker?		
Demonstrate a physiological, (e.g., body language) and psychological response?		
Exhibit empathy rather than sympathy?		
Exhibit with verbal and nonverbal cues that build bridges rather than walls between the project manager and the speaker?		
Seek feedback on your response?		

Chapter 5

Preparing the Communications Management Plan and Establishing an Issues Management Process

---

Effective communications just does not happen like an idle conversation with a stranger on a street corner. Rather, it is a directed, conscious effort to get people to share thoughts, feelings, and information in a manner that achieves a common vision. The communications management plan (CMP) and the issues management process (IMP) are the tools for doing so.

Contributions of the Project Management Information System (PMIS)

A PMIS can contribute to a CMP. It can help identify who are the major stakeholders on a project and the role they play. A PMIS may contain, for example, a project charter, a statement of work, historical data from previous projects, or organization charts. Using such information can help project managers draft a CMP replete with the necessary information.

It can also contribute to an IMP by providing a historical database of issues that have arisen on similar projects and how project managers addressed them; memos and minutes from previous meetings that may have provided direction on how issues should be managed; and project policies and procedures that provide relevant guidance and direction.

Communications Management Plan

A CMP is a formal document that identifies the communications goals, objectives, and requirements of a project. It also designates who is responsible for communicating the right information to the right people at the right time in the right format and in the right quantity and quality.

A CMP has two purposes. The first one is to acquire the right information and send it to the right people in the right form at the right time. Doing so requires engaging the right people, selecting the right medium, and conveying the appropriate data or information. The second purpose is to ensure that the communication process occurs and sustains itself throughout the life of a project.

Characteristics

An effective CMP has several characteristics.

1. A CMP is documented to varying levels of breadth, depth, and formality to satisfy the requirements of a project. For small, simple projects, a voluminous CMP may be unnecessary; however, for a large complex project, it may require considerable breadth, depth, and formality (i.e., documented), and cover a large range of topics (i.e., meetings, reports).
2. It is written clearly, like any other project documentation. The document reflects good writing practices and describes communications needs clearly.
3. A CMP is concise. The contents include only what is necessary to define, plan, execute, control, and close a project from a communications perspective. It is also geared towards the specific needs of stakeholders.
4. A CMP is comprehensive. It provides adequate coverage of information for people to contribute toward achieving the overall vision of their projects. A CMP can be concise as well as simultaneously comprehensive by providing sufficient breadth and depth of coverage.
5. A CMP is accessible by all the people who need to reference it. It is not a document that should sit on a shelf, available only to a chosen few. In today's highly computerized environment, accessibility should be the one restriction.

The challenge is in determining which stakeholders should have access to the CMP.

6. It must have the commitment of the people affected by it. Stakeholders should buy off on the document to get them to abide by the contents. Without buy-off, the chances increase that no one will adhere to the content. The CMP then becomes nothing more than mere formality.

Challenges

Developing a communications plan, although conceptually simple, is not easy to make a reality. Project managers face several challenges.

Size: Principally, this involves a number of people. The more people, the greater the number of different interactions that can occur among the stakeholders, creating a complex web of interaction. The number of relationships increases dramatically with the number of people on a project. For example, project managers may want to add more people to a complex set of tasks to improve progress. This approach may backfire because additional people increase the number of interactions and the need for people to communicate more frequently as they get up to speed.

Complexity: This challenge pertains to meeting technical requirements. The more technically complex a project the greater the chances for miscommunications and lack of communications to occur. Multidisciplinary teams often start expressing themselves in jargon defined and understood differently by the various parties. They often are less engaged in interaction with other people because of the solitary nature of their work. Specialists often require the time to think and work alone. A situation may arise when these people find themselves temporarily isolated from others, especially on knowledge-based projects. This isolation, although important, can result in less interaction with others, creating a wide communications chasm among team members. Not only are interactions minimal, but when they communicate, they use terminology that others find hard to understand.

Location: Location considers whether team members are colocated or dispersed across a wide geographical area. It is perhaps the biggest challenge confronting an effective communications plan. The more people are dispersed, the greater the challenge in getting them to communicate regularly. The likelihood of communications failures and miscommunication will increase. Geography can attenuate communications channels for a multitude of reasons. Different time zones can augment the difficulties of a project with stakeholders spread across a continent and around the world. In today's global environment, many project managers find this challenge quite frequently. People may be spread across a continent or several continents. The distance, coupled with language and cultural barriers, makes communications difficult even when using the best communications technology. Communications can become infrequent, and when it does occur can become quite frustrating.

Diversity: Diversity recognizes that people are different in many ways. Common differences are, of course, race, religion, and sex. Project managers, however, frequently overlook others. Diversity can manifest itself through cultural differences, thinking and working styles, and communication approaches. This type of diversity provides plenty of opportunity for positive and negative conflicts. Getting people to communicate from this perspective can prove quite challenging because they see and approach reality differently, thereby complicating interaction and communication. Globalization can exacerbate this challenge. For example, some cultures prefer communicating on a more personal level, whereas others have no problem communicating electronically. Many times, project managers find themselves frustrated over sending e-mails to foreign partners explaining solutions to problems that exist. Still, the foreign partners do not comprehend the instructions. The reasons may be many, but often the foreign partners work better with face-to-face interaction because that is their primary mode of communication. Even with the use of videoconferencing, communications can fail.

Technology: The types of technological tools are extensive and include fax, e-mail, videoconferencing, teleconferencing, Web conferencing, microcomputers, and satellites. Technology can be used as a tool to communicate effectively by adapting it to the user's preferred working style. The power of this technology is reflected in the rise of telecommuting and working virtually.

Technology, however, does not guarantee effective communications. Some people, especially ones with less than desirable interpersonal skills, for example, will use technology as a means to escape communicating with others. They will do whatever they can to minimize face-to-face interaction or even avoid meetings. Dialogue is virtually nonexistent, and their participation at specific meetings is lukewarm at best. On a large project, the following scenario is not uncommon: Two people sitting in cubicles on the same floor do not like one another. They might communicate solely via e-mail. On occasion, one of them may say he never received a certain e-mail from the other, knowing all too well the truth is otherwise. Ironically, the e-mails often are poorly constructed and wordy, only adding to more communications problems.

Norms: This challenge is reflected in patterns of behavior. Norms provide consistency in thought and behavior, and are both their strength and weakness. Norms provide consistency because people know what is expected of them and how they should interact. Norms can sometimes impede the ability to adapt new patterns of behavior and communication. Deviating from the norm can result in lack of participation by certain stakeholders. A perfect example is a team that gets set in its way. The team may be doing well but is not open to new ideas regarding processes or products. Even the introduction of a new tool can prove threatening. Under this scenario, the best approaches to knowledge transfer and sharing cannot overcome obstacles, especially if the team feels threatened.

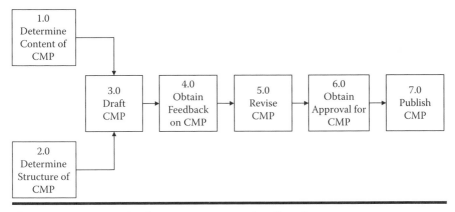

Figure 5.1   Communications management plan flowchart.

Making the CMP a Reality

Developing, deploying, and maintaining a CMP is quite easy. Following these simple guidelines will help project managers improve the chances of having an effective CMP for their project (Figure 5.1).

Determine the structure and content of the CMP. Although it can vary in structure, a CMP generally has the following outline and content:

A. Purpose of the CMP
B. Scope
C. Objectives
D. Constraints (overall)
E. Table addressing:
    a. Approach
    b. Goals
    c. Participants
    d. Medium
    e. Agenda
    f. Responsibilities
    g. Frequency and time
    h. Equipment and supplies
    i. Linkage
    j. Constraints
    k. Comments

Purpose: This section provides a short description of the project and how the communications plan can help achieve its vision. For example: "The project will achieve these goals: compliance with Section 404 of the Sarbanes-Oxley Act by February 28 and identify opportunities for consolidating systems and processes. This communications plan will describe the processes, tools, and techniques for accomplishing these goals."

Scope: This section describes the extent of the communications plan (e.g., regularly scheduled meetings), as opposed to what it doesn't cover (e.g., ad hoc meetings) between two people working on an issue. This section is often combined with the purpose. Example: This plan does not cover ad hoc working meetings to resolve technical issues, but does cover ongoing meetings, such as project status reviews.

Objectives: The objectives section describes what the CMP hopes to accomplish. Like the scope, it can be covered in the purpose. Example: This plan will ensure that all meetings and their attendees have been identified. It will also identify the major reports that must be identified weekly and who must prepare and reserve them.

Constraints: This section describes some of the restrictions the project manager might confront in executing the CMP. The constraints may be, for instance, any technological ones or geographic locations of team members. A useful addition to this section is to highlight some of the communications tools and techniques employed to deal with these constraints. Example: Where possible, emphasis will be on conducting meetings remotely using teleconferencing and Webex technology.

Table: The table is the "meat" of the CMP. This section covers the breadth and depth of the CMP and provides details for each communications approach. Just about all columns are optional, with the exception of the approach column. Here is a list of items that may be included in the table: approach, goals, participants, medium, agenda, responsibilities frequency, time, equipment and supplies, linkage, constraints, and comments.

The *approach column* contains the name and description of each communications event or activity that occurs. This event or activity might include, for example, a steering committee report or a project review meeting.

The *goals column* describes what the event or activity hopes to achieve. These goals might include sharing information or dealing with a change to the schedule baseline.

The *participants column* lists the stakeholders involved. The list may include simply the names of organizations or specific people. Being specific is preferred, of course.

The *medium column* lists the tools and techniques to achieve the goals. Examples in this column might include a meeting, written report, or an e-mail to certain stakeholders, Web conferencing, or placing output on a Web site.

The *agenda column* lists the major categories of topics to be covered. The agenda for a standard meeting might reflect, for example, what is always covered and allow for topics that arise, based upon needs at the time.

The *responsibilities column* lists the major activities to ensure that they will happen as planned. For example, someone may be assigned responsibility for ensuring that a meeting room is fully equipped with supplies or that he or she acts as a facilitator or scribe.

The *frequency and time column* lists how often the communications occurs and when. Typical items listed might include ad hoc, every other Thursday, or bi-weekly on a specific day.

The *equipment and supplies column* highlights any specific support requirements to execute whatever approach is taken. These items might include software, microcomputer, white boards, easel pads and stands, projectors, markers, lighting, and other hardware equipment.

The *linkage column* lists any approaches taken by this project in association with other projects. For example, a project might feed information to another project. It is important to ensure that whatever communications approach taken for the current project is tied, for example, to a related, downstream, or concurrent project. This linkage might include feeding information to generate additional reports or making decisions at key meetings and communicating results to another project. This linkage is especially important in programs.

The *constraints column* lists some of the factors that restrict the performance of an approach listed in the CMP. Constraints might include reports being generated or distributed in a specific format (e.g., hard copy vs. digital) or that certain people must attend certain meetings. The additional *comments column* covers anything else that may relate to an identified approach. Examples might include ground rules for meetings, specific report decks to generate, and approvals for certain decisions.

Draft the CMP. Drafting the CMP can occur in one of two ways. Project managers can draft the initial version and have other key stakeholders review it, or they can assemble all the key stakeholders in a room and provide content to it. Obviously, the former approach takes less time but may invite extensive criticism of the draft, whereas the latter takes more time but obviates criticism.

Obtain feedback. The CMP is a living document, meaning that it will require updates throughout the life cycle of a project. Stakeholders and the means of communication will constantly change. A good practice is to review the CMP with stakeholders periodically to obtain this feedback.

Revise the CMP. Using the feedback, project managers can make the necessary updates to the content of the CMP. An important point here is to keep configuration control over the CMP to ensure that everyone references the same document.

Obtain approval for the CMP. A CMP should go through a rigorous approval process to ensure the accuracy of the content. Key stakeholders should give approval for updates to the document.

Publish the CMP. Upon receiving approval, project managers can publish the CMP. They can do so simply by posting the document on a server or Web site. The document at that location can serve as the authoritative CMP for the project.

CMP Implementation Suggestions

As mentioned earlier, developing a CMP plan is relatively easy. Implementing one can present a challenge. Here are some suggestions for implementing an effective CMP on a project:

1. Establish an issues governance process. The purpose of this process is to identify issues, give them visibility, and track their resolution. The key is to give visibility to the issues, such as posting them in a critical issues/action item log on a Web site, sending the log out to all team members, and following up on them during meetings.

2. Escalate the issues. This suggestion is closely tied to the last point but involves more of a way to overcome an impasse with a stakeholder. By creating a help-needed list of items that you can present to a steering committee or to senior management, you at least put pressure on noncompliant stakeholders. Noncompliance can take many forms, such as nonattendance at meetings, not providing status for reports, or disrupting sessions. This visibility can continue until the issue has been resolved.

3. Recognize that the medium does make a difference. Project managers should employ a medium to gain the desired effect if this option is available to them. For example, critical meetings might not be best served by a teleconference but rather through face-to-face meetings. Another example might be providing hard-copy reports to have a more dramatic effect than sending an electronic copy.

4. Role identification can prove helpful. For example, assigning someone as the single point of contact for leading discussions on certain topics (e.g., technical issues) at meetings can engender a greater sense of responsibility to participate. Responsibility assigned to items listed in critical issues and action items can also prove meaningful. Segregating roles at meetings (e.g., scribe, facilitator) can also generate commitment to execute a particular role.

5. Give visibility to results. For meetings, ensure that the minutes get posted on a Web site or distributed. For performance reports, ensure that the results get similar visibility. Regardless of approach, ensure that the right people at the right time receive the results in the most appropriate format. The key is to give people the visibility that they want and, just as important, that they hope to avoid.

6. Gain feedback and follow up on results. Just because someone agrees with something at a meeting or the content of a report that shows erroneous or negative performance (e.g., SPI less than 1.0), it does not mean that the work of a CMP is complete. Project managers must ensure that feedback and follow-up occurs. Visibility can only go so far, and then project managers must employ dogged determination to ensure that all the approaches of a CMP have been successfully deployed.

Figure 5.2 Issues management flowchart.

Issues Management Process

Issues management process (IMP) is a formal approach to identifying, analyzing, and addressing concerns or problems not originally appearing in the project plan (Figure 5.2). It provides a means for managing events and issues without having to replan.

From time to time, issues arise that can affect the outcome of project results. The management of these issues, whether they relate to cost, schedule, or quality, will determine to a large degree whether stakeholders, including project managers, can manage issues more effectively by following these guidelines.

Establish an issues management process. A governance process, as mentioned earlier, has the purpose of identifying issues and making them viable. At a minimum, the issues management process should enable the project team to capture issues, determine their relevance and importance, track completion status, and add any relevant information.

Escalate issues. An issues management process should provide an opportunity for all stakeholders to present issues and have them recorded. The typical venue for these issues is the project review meetings. During these meetings, stakeholders can present issues or query the status of the existing ones. Under some circumstances, stakeholders may find that certain issues must be escalated beyond the purview of the project. A process must be in place, therefore, that allows the team to elevate issues to higher levels of management. Often, such issues are placed on a help-needed log or slide or in an activity report that is submitted to members of a steering committee.

Give visibility to issues. Project managers have several options for giving visibility to issues. They can cover them at the project status review meetings or post an issues log on a project Web site. The key is to keep issues, especially the critical ones, in the forefront of the stakeholders until resolved.

Obtain feedback. Project status review meetings are perfect venues for receiving feedback on the resolution of issues. Other approaches include obtaining feedback via e-mail or even a telephone call. If these two approaches are used, however, project managers should populate the critical issues lists prior to the project status review.

Follow up on results. Just because people say they have addressed a critical issue does not necessarily mean they did so very effectively (Figure 5.3). Sometimes, issues resurface. The best preventive approach is to revisit a completed issue from time to time to ascertain whether the solution was effective and not merely a short-term fix.

No.	Description	Responsibility	Date	Committed Date	Completed Date	Comments

Figure 5.3   Critical issues/action item log.

Issues Management Challenges

Implementation of an IMP poses two challenges.

The first is getting people to participate in the process. The major reason behind this challenge is that people often do not raise an issue for fear of being assigned responsibility for resolving it. The solution is to encourage someone other than the person identifying the issue to take this responsibility.

Another challenge is follow-up on the contents. Sometimes, during the intensity of a project, the issues can become lost or forgotten. Project managers can deal with this consistently and persistently by going over issues, for example, at status review meetings.

Significant Contributor

A CMP and an IMP are essential for any project. Failure to produce either is a failure in communications. Of course, both can vary in the degree of formality. Regardless, both are integral contributors to the success of any project simply because they help to ensure contributions from all those engaged in the process.

Getting Started Checklist			
Question		*Yes*	*No*
1.	Does your CMP have these characteristics:		
	Accessible?		
	Comprehensive?		
	Concise?		
	Have the commitment from the people affected by it?		
	Have the necessary level of breadth, depth, and formality?		
	Written clearly?		
2.	Do you consider these challenges when developing the CMP:		
	Complexity?		
	Diversity?		
	Location?		
	Norms?		
	Size?		
	Technology?		
3.	For the CMP, do you:		
	Determine a considerations structure such as:		
	Constraints?		
	Content?		
	Goals?		
	Objectives?		
	Purpose?		
	Scope?		
	For each communications approach (e.g., meetings, reports):		
	Agenda, if applicable?		
	Comments?		
	Constraints?		
	Description?		
	Equipment, if applicable?		
	Frequency?		
	Linkage?		
	Medium?		
	Objectives?		
	Participants?		

Getting Started Checklist (Continued)			
Question		*Yes*	*No*
	Responsibilities?		
	Supplies, if applicable?		
	Time?		
4.	When implementing a CMP, do you consider these suggestions:		
	Escalate any issues?		
	Establish an issues governance process?		
	Give feedback and follow up on results?		
	Give visibility to results?		
	Identify roles?		
	Recognize that the medium does make a difference?		
5.	When considering Issues Management (IM), do you perform these steps:		
	Define the necessary processes?		
	Escalate issues related to the CMP?		
	Obtain feedback?		
	Follow up on results?		
6.	If you decide to use a Critical Issues/Action Item Log, do you consider these entries:		
	Number?		
	Description?		
	Responsibility?		
	Date?		
	Committed Date?		
	Completed Date?		
	Comments?		
7.	For IM, do you address these challenges:		
	Following up on the contents in the log?		
	Getting people to participate in the process?		

Chapter 6

Drafting and Publishing Documentation

Project managers, as communicators, must write effectively, but like many people, they may feel threatened by the act of writing. Yet writing is a reality on projects, whether using e-mail, creating Microsoft PowerPoint slides, or developing procedures. Project managers cannot escape this task.

Contributions of the Project Management Information System (PMIS)

A PMIS can provide a wealth of data and information for preparing project documentation, consisting of text, numbers, and graphics; data feeds from other systems, if available; and an audit trail of performance and events that have occurred. The PMIS also provides a consistent guide for stakeholders to identify the interrelationships among the content when drafting and publishing documentation.

Why Writing Matters

Writing plays an important role on projects for several reasons.

First, project managers are communicating at least 90 percent of their work day. The best approach for doing so is through correspondence, regardless of the tool. When meetings are impossible, project managers will likely have to craft documentation for use as reference material.

Second, documentation provides an effective audit trail of the decisions and actions taken on a project. This audit trail does more than satisfy auditors and compliance requirements; it provides continuity from one phase to the next. Project managers often must ensure that they document key decisions and actions.

Third, documentation provides for knowledge transfer. In many environments, turnover is high. Documentation can help effectively capture data, information, and knowledge to mitigate the impacts of this turnover. Project managers will likely have to prepare most of the project management documentation. However, they will also have to play a key role in overseeing the quality of documentation produced by others.

Fourth, documentation—whether in hard or soft copy—will require writing. The quality of the writing in documentation will reflect on the quality of work by the project manager and his or her team. Documentation replete with misspellings and grammatical errors will, for example, diminish the value of the content from the perspective of the readers.

Fifth, documentation is a means to protect oneself. Project managers depend on many stakeholders for support. Well-written documentation enables them to capture any agreements or decisions with key stakeholders. When they use documentation for protection, project managers need to ensure that the contents are clear, concise, and grammatically correct. Otherwise, the documentation may not prove credible as a means of protection.

Too Little Importance

Unfortunately, many projects managers place very little importance on the quality of their documentation. A random review of their documentation, whether e-mail or project procedures, will likely reveal the characteristics of being wordy, imprecise, unclear, irrelevant (e.g., outdated and incorrect content), and voluminous (e.g., superfluous content). In addition, the content likely flows illogically, not focused on the readers.

Generally, project managers who cannot write well may be poor communicators in all other modes of communication, e.g., giving presentations too. Because they spend a large amount of time trying to get their ideas across, some project managers may spend 90 percent of their time not doing their job as well as they might.

Project managers should strive, therefore, to produce documentation that is clear, concise, concrete, relevant, specific, and has an appealing appearance.

Project Manager as Writer

So how do project managers determine whether they are effective writers?

One approach is through the use of a readability index. Several indices exist, such as the Fog Index and the Flesch–Kincaid Indices. These and other indices help provide project managers with an idea of the clarity and conciseness of their work; however, they do not convey how well the content satisfies their readers' needs. They simply address readability levels from an educational level. Project managers, too, often lack the time to apply these indices unless they have software to perform calculations to derive an index.

The best approach to determine the readability and usefulness of documentation is to ask an intended user to review it prior to its publication. End recipients are the best judges of whether the document in general and its content in particular are clear. A good rule of thumb is that if the reader must revisit a paragraph or an entire document to understand it, then rewriting is necessary. Formal, even informal, reviews are the best ways to determine whether a document meets the characteristics of clarity, conciseness, relevance, and audience tailoring.

Project managers, as writers, must possess several skills and talents:

Good technical knowledge. This knowledge enables them to craft documents with meaningful content. Having a really solid knowledge of a topic poses, however, some challenges. Project managers can lose focus on the readership, creating unnecessary content that is riddled with jargon.

Communications. They must be able to create documentation in the prevailing work group language (e.g., English). On a multicultural project, however, not everyone may have adequate competence in that language, and they should carefully consider word choice when crafting documentation. In some cases, a few members of a team may not be fluent in the prevailing language. Project managers might find it worthwhile to have documentation translated for them. Although numbers are universal, however, words lend themselves to misinterpretation. Translation of documents, such as weekly written status reports and project procedures, may prove helpful.

Interpersonal. More often than not, project managers must be able to extract data and information from other people to craft documentation. To do so requires having the ability to relate to people to extract what they need using effective and active listening skills. Other related skills include the ability to conduct informative interviews to meet their needs.

Incidentally, good interpersonal skills require developing an appreciation for different communication and information processing styles of people. By understanding these styles, project managers can exercise versatility when creating documentation that suits the needs of the readers. For example, some people are very visually oriented, whereas others prefer text; others prefer a very detailed view, whereas some take a more general, systemic view.

Research. Project managers must be able to define and find exactly what they need. They must have the ability to focus with determination. Without both of these abilities, they will find it very difficult to complete documentation. Fortunately, in the contemporary environment, many project managers have access to research material thanks to the Internet and intranets. Web-based technology has enabled project managers to have access to almost real-time data and information that can prove useful for developing documentation. Indeed, this ability to access data and information may obviate the need to create documentation because it already exists.

Organizational skills. They must have the ability to logically arrange ideas and content to satisfy the needs of readers. One of the basic skills of a project manager is to have good organizational skills. These skills are directly transferable to the development of documentation. Project managers must be able to take the data and information from diffuse resources and arrange it in a way ensuring that readers will understand the contents of a document and apply it directly to their environment. Writing meaningful status reports and procedures are examples that require solid organizational skills.

Documentation Phases

Preparing documentation often occurs in phases, some in parallel and others in sequence. Regardless of order, the phases are: draft, review, revise, approve, distribute, and maintain (Figure 6.1).

Draft

Draft is preparing a document. A document can go through several drafts before it is ready for review. Drafting a document can consume 60–70 percent of the effort put into its life cycle but may involve 30–40 percent of the duration of its life cycle.

The draft phase consists of several actions that can occur in just about any order:

- Defining the readers
- Determining goals
- Conducting research
- Preparing an outline
- Creating the document
- Conducting the review
- Revising the manuscript
- Receiving approval/disapproval
- Publishing and distributing the document
- Maintaining and updating the document

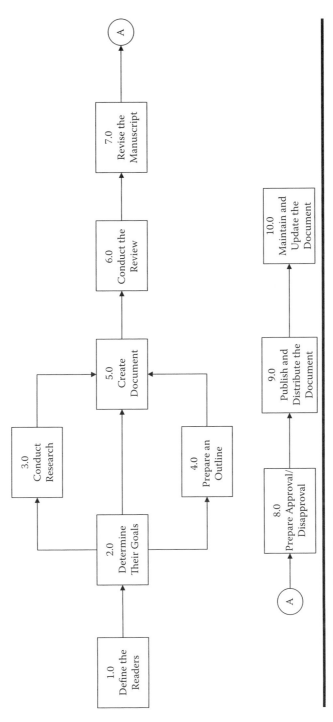

Figure 6.1 Documentation flowchart.

Defining Readers

Of all the actions, this one is the most important. Project managers must determine which stakeholders will read the document. This drives the content and the level of detail. Some stakeholders, such as senior executives, will require a wider breadth of content and less detail than others, such as team members, who will likely require a narrower focus and more detail. Failure to define the readership upfront can result in producing documentation that may satisfy no one but the writer.

Determining Goals

With the readership defined, project managers must next ascertain the goals and objectives of the documentation. For example, is the documentation used not only to inform but to explain or persuade? Is it to serve as an audit trail? Or is it to enable someone to perform a set of tasks?

An ancillary to ascertaining the goals of the documentation is the determination of its scope, or more specifically, what is in and out of its scope. Defining the scope enables reducing the breadth of the content and even the level of detail.

Conducting Research

Not all data and information will likely be readily available. With the audience defined and the corresponding goals for the documentation, project managers can then ascertain what is or is not readily available.

Project managers have several modes of research at their disposal. One mode is to review existing documentation and data sources. As a project progresses through its life cycle the amount of documentation and number of data sources increase, making the tasks of the project managers easier. In the earlier phases of a project life cycle, the likelihood of unavailable sources is higher, thereby requiring more imagination and determination. Nevertheless, project managers must always question the validity and reliability of the content of sources for the simple reason that bad data can result in poor information that can have, in turn, negative performance results.

Another mode is to conduct interviews with people who can provide the necessary data and information for documentation. Interviews can prove useful for preparing documentation if project managers follow a few guidelines.

The first one is to prepare for the interview. Project managers must know their requirements for data and information and the questions to ask. Going into an interview ill prepared often translates into poor results, that is, not satisfying the project managers' requirements for data and information. Preparation for an interview requires defining at a high level the who, what, when, where, why, and hows. This preparation will enable project managers to feel more in control of the interview session.

The second guideline is to determine the type of questions to be asked. Structured questions are helpful for obtaining precise answers, usually offering a dichotomous choice. Open-ended questions provide a means to expand on what the interviewee said or to uncover underlying pieces of data and information. The ideal approach is to use both types of questions; having more or less of either type does not matter. Project managers' data and information requirements should determine the best mix of questions and the availability of time for the interview session. An example of an open-ended question might be something like: "What do you think is the cause for the slide of the milestone?" An example of a structured question requiring a specific answer: "What is the overall schedule performance index for the project?"

The third guideline is to conduct an interview away from the interviewee's locus of activity (unless it is absolutely necessary). The reason is that the interviewee will be too distracted and, consequently, find it difficult to focus on the purpose of the interview session. Try to have the session away from work activity so that the interviewee does not find his attention diverted to the needs of someone else—for example, a colleague.

The fourth guideline is to focus on the purpose of the interview. A tendency is for the interviewer and interviewee to stray to other topics. The onus is on project managers to keep the interview focused on the topic. A solid focus on the desired results of the interview will help maintain focus. During an interview session, project managers may be forced to ask specific questions that interviewees may not want to think about, such as significant tasks in the schedule. Rather than receive a direct answer, some project managers, to avoid confrontation, will settle for a discussion about an allied subject or the symptoms. They must remain focused on getting the answers that they need by bringing the interviewee back on track either through additional questions or forceful comments stressing the need to focus.

The fifth guideline is to provide the interviewee with some idea of the types of questions the project managers will ask. Interviewees can then formulate their thoughts and have some data and information available for the session. In some cases, project managers may want to send out questions in advance. By doing so, interviewees can perform research or collect data and information and have it available at the interview session. Or, they can do their homework and send the results, and project managers can use all the data and information to ask additional questions.

The sixth guideline is to apply effective and active listening skills during the session. Project managers may have certain prejudices, but they should avoid letting them surface during the interview. They should also avoid giving physical and verbal expressions that persuade interviewees to hesitate in providing information. The objective is to maintain independence while acquiring the necessary data and information. Being an effective and active listener is to have two critical skills. Unfortunately, project managers with these two skills are quite rare. Instead, the tendency exists for project managers to think that they have to come up with all the answers themselves. The results often prove dismal because these project managers hear only what they want and not what they need to hear.

Preparing an Outline

This activity serves multiple purposes. First, it helps the writer to logically organize the data and information. Second, it allows the writer to focus on the readers. Project managers can then trim any data and information that do not satisfy needs or goals of the readers. Third, it forces clarity of thought for project managers because the logical format will reveal any inconsistencies with ideas and content. Finally, it serves as a communications tool for project managers to use when meeting with readers to determine whether the document is eventually relevant, contains sufficient detail and, ultimately, is of value. The challenge with an outline is like any activity on a project; project managers should provide the time and exert the willpower to do it. Too often, project managers, like many unseasoned writers, jump towards developing a document first and then making needless content and structural changes.

Creating the Document

As mentioned earlier, the readership of documentation will determine substantially the type and level of content. Regardless of the readers, project managers will want to achieve several goals with their documentation.

Project managers should be direct and to the point, both in terms of content and words. Adding too much of either will confuse the readers and lead them to ignore it and seek what they need elsewhere.

The challenge is to be complete without overkill. That is, project managers should provide enough information to satisfy readers' requirements, not less. Providing too little content can be, however, as bad as providing too much.

Content should be written clearly. Readers should not have to read a sentence repeatedly for understanding. Each sentence should communicate with minimum verbiage. Trying to become a literary giant can turn off rather than engage readers (Figure 6.2).

Be specific in your choice of language. Using, for instance, many adverbs can confuse a reader. Terms like "many times" or "occasionally" do not strengthen but weaken communication.

Use a combination of analysis and synthesis. Analysis, in this context, means dividing content into manageable components. Synthesis means taking the manageable components and reassembling them into a meaningful construct. For example, using analysis and synthesis can help the project manager and reader to better comprehend content and arrange it logically. Then, the project manager can

To: Ted Wellis   June 11, 2012

Cc: Cindy Sanderford

Subject: Follow-up on Status Inquiry

Last Thursday, July 26, you inquired about the accuracy of the current schedule date for Task 1043, Build Module 7A.

You were right. A discrepancy existed between what you said was the remaining hours and what appeared in the data base. This discrepancy did not, however, impact the critical path.

Although we were unable to determine as of yet the cause of the discrepancy, the planner and I made the necessary adjustments to the data base and recalculated your portion of the schedule. Attached is the revised report. Please review it for accuracy.

If you have any questions, please contact me via e-mail or by phone.

Sandy Kauffman
Project Manager
123-7890 Ext. 98

Figure 6.2   Example of a well-written memo.

experiment in a way that augments comprehension of the material while minimizing rework.

Be objective. Most project documentation is not a persuasive essay. Rather, it provides useful, meaningful information for readers to act upon. The minute a project manager attempts to add biases into content, such as ancillary comments, the reader may formulate mental blocks that hinder receptivity to the message.

As mentioned earlier, one of the best ways to determine whether documentation meets the preceding characteristics is to have readers provide feedback. The project manager can then make the necessary changes using that feedback.

Most documentation, whether a policy, procedure, presentation, or some other form of narrative documentation, consists of three parts: introduction, discussion, and conclusion.

Introduction. This section constitutes about 5–10 percent of the content of a document and includes some or all of the following information: purpose, what is within the scope of the section and what isn't, background information, and related documentation.

The introduction is important for several reasons: (1) it gives readers an idea about a topic so they can determine whether it meets his or her needs, (2) it provides a "big picture" prior to delving into the details, and (3) it grabs the readers' attention and entices them to continue reading.

Discussion. This section constitutes about 80–90 percent of the documentation. It communicates detail, and does so logically. This detail can follow different patterns:

- *Problem–solution.* The content describes one or more problems and then provides one or more solutions.
- *Chronology.* The material is presented according to a time sequence that often culminates in a product or service.
- *Spatial arrangement.* The material is presented according to location or geography. The sequence often results in a product or service.
- *Comparison and contrast.* Two or more dissimilar topics are discussed in a manner reflecting differences and similarities.
- *Process description.* Process description often takes the format of input, process, and output. Content, such as data, is manipulated and converted into output, such as information.
- *Definitions.* Often, this is called a "glossary"; however, definitions may be captured within a document in other ways.
- *Topical.* Topics are covered according to some order, such as complex to simple or most to least important.
- *Conditional.* This one usually takes an if/then construct. "If" is the condition; "then" is the consequent.
- *Issues, facts, and conclusions.* The project manager describes a series of issues, with each one followed with supporting facts, and then conclusions.
- *Stakeholder or customer.* The project manager groups content, for example, by relevance to people or organizations.
- *Conclusion.* Like the introduction, a conclusion consists of 5–10 percent of the content. Like the introduction, too, it provides the big picture. The difference between the two is that the introduction provides an overall picture and then leads to the details; the conclusion takes the details and then provides the big picture. A conclusion may reiterate the main points, call for additional action, or both. It may also direct the reader to other sources of information.

All written documentation should follow style considerations, which fall into five categories: clarity, conciseness, relevancy, constructiveness, and appropriateness.

Clarity. This consideration is very important and relates to narrative description and layout of material. Project managers can achieve clarity by keeping adverbs and adjectives to a minimum, using conversational English, avoiding the use of foreign words and jargon, defining acronyms, writing in active rather than passive voice, and eradicating any double negatives. They can also improve clarity in layout by providing plenty of white space on a page. Readers often view large blocks of text as tedious in finding the information they need. Additional layout considerations include using graphics, such as tables, to communicate data and information. Be sure graphics integrate with text to avoid distracting the reader from the principal thoughts of the writer.

Conciseness. "Less is best" is the motto here. Generally, project managers should understate rather than overstate. The reader will indicate if more content is necessary. Like clarity, conciseness is achieved on two levels: narrative description and layout, but this time in ideas. Project managers can achieve conciseness by minimizing the number of words for narrative text; choosing specific, concrete words; and avoid interjecting needless phrases (i.e., clichés). They can also achieve conciseness by presenting ideas and facts logically without coming across as convoluted, contradictory, or repetitive. Their objective is to communicate their ideas, supported with the right amount of data and information. If ideas and supporting material appear in multiple places, for example, readers may experience confusion or find the content superfluous.

Relevance. This category adds to clarity and conciseness by improving content and comprehension. The best approach to achieve relevance is to focus on the reader. This focus will enable the project manager to determine whether to add or remove material. In other words, determine what is within and what exceeds the scope of the document.

Here are several heuristics to help achieve relevancy.

- *Group related ideas together.* That is, keep ideas together that share similarity (e.g., characteristics) in one or more paragraphs. Move dissimilar ideas to a different section of a text or remove.
- *Organize content in order of importance.* By doing so, the project manager can then determine the content to provide and discard any "insignificant" ideas. Developing an outline can help exercise these two heuristics. After building the outline, a project manager can more easily organize the ideas and then discard content even before writing.
- *Augment text with graphics.* Too often, project managers put graphics in a document without referencing it in the text, creating a disconnection between the two. When that happens, people find it difficult to determine their relevancy to each other, breaking the reader's concentration.

Keep one idea per paragraph. Adding multiple ideas in a paragraph can confuse a reader by enticing him or her to shift focus too quickly and not see the connection. Ideas should have their own paragraphs.

Constructiveness. The overall style of a document can influence how well a reader accepts material. In other words, the overall tone of a document influences the way the material comes across to the reader. Here are some heuristics for improving the tone of any document:

- State material positively rather than negatively. Write material that avoids words like "not," for example. At best, keep the material neutral by avoiding adjectives and adverbs that only add vague qualifications.
- Be conservative in tone by minimizing literary devices. Avoiding foreign words and jargon are two good ways to improve comprehension.
- Emphasize facts and data to avoid creating a mental block in the reader's mind. This heuristic especially applies to project management documentation. Project managers should avoid placing their opinions in text unless circumstances demand it; otherwise, they may turn off the reader.
- Use parallelism for related ideas when constructing sentences. Parallel structure for material enables a reader to comprehend material. For related ideas, for example, start sentences in each paragraph with an action verb rather than with a propositional phrase.
- Use plenty of white space. This heuristic addresses the layout of an entire document. Use white space to draw attention to a particular idea in a document. Large blocks of text can bury an idea and fatigue the reader.
- Give preference to simple construction over the complex. Long, complex, and convoluted sentences lose the reader. Simple constructions allow readers to better identify and comprehend main ideas. In other words, use the simple construct of subject–verb–object.

Appropriateness. This category centers on proper grammar. The rules for grammar are extensive, and many are beyond the scope of simple documentation writing; however, some deserve mentioning. For a more advanced listing of these rules, refer to one of the many grammar books in print. Here are five common grammatical rules to follow when preparing documentation for projects. These rules are the ones that many project managers violate frequently.

- Spell out all acronyms initially, followed by the acronym in parentheses. Avoid assuming a reader will know what they represent, let alone what they mean.
- Avoid mixing passive and active voice. Too often, project managers mix the two, leading to a lack of clarity, and, consequently, confuse the reader. Although preference is towards active over passive voice, project managers use either one but do so consistently throughout the text.
- Place adverbs and adjectives close to the modified word. Adjectives and adverbs that "float" adrift in a sentence cause a reader to lose his or her focus.
- Use consistent tense for verbs used throughout a paragraph and, in most cases, an entire document. If a project manager uses present tense, then maintain present tense. If he or she must shift to another tense (e.g., past tense), then do so only to emphasize a point.

- Subject and verb should match. A plural subject requires choosing a verb that matches the plurality of the subject. This rule also applies to using pronouns in a sentence.
- Apply standard conventions to the layout of a document. These conventions include having a heading and subtitles to enable referencing of content and following the logic. Also use consistent margins throughout a document. The citing of references should follow a consistent pattern.

Essentially, the overall rule is to give preference to simplicity over complexity, regarding sentence construction by following the basic sentence structure of subject–verb–object. Avoid using elaborate punctuation.

Conducting the Review

Once comfortable with the draft of a document, a project manager can submit it for review to obtain feedback. Sending out a document for review serves several purposes. First, reviewers provide a fresh "set of eyes" looking at the document, enabling them to detect flaws from content to grammatical errors. Second, reviewers discover the most meaningful content to them and, subsequently, enabling a project manager to pare content. Third, and perhaps most important, reviewers will exhibit less resistance to a document upon its release as it becomes their document, too. They will have a sense of ownership, thereby minimizing their criticism.

During a revision process project managers must be "hard skinned" by removing their ego. In other words, avoid defensiveness when receiving feedback; otherwise, readers will become reticent and will not give the candid feedback that is being sought. Project managers do not have to incorporate feedback but they need to listen and consider it.

A project manager can take one or more of these three approaches for conducting a review: serial, concurrent, or group.

A serial review requires each reader to review a document one person at a time. The principal advantage of a serial review is that each reader has the opportunity to see the comments and suggestions of previous reviewers. The principal disadvantage is that it is time consuming, waiting for the document to move from one reviewer to the next.

Concurrent review requires sending out multiple copies to reviewers. The principal advantage is that it reduces the flow time. The disadvantage is a project manager must juggle multiple manuscripts or files and then reconcile revisions.

Group review requires interactive participation from everyone at one time, such as by using a bridge line or conference call, or assembling in a room. The principal advantage of this approach is that everyone at once can provide their feedback as the project manager captures it. The other advantage is that the project manager can ask questions to the validity of feedback by piggy-backing off the insights of attendees. A principal disadvantage is that disagreement over content or even a phrase may require several sessions, increasing the flow time for completing a document.

Due to information technology, concurrent reviews are more common and ease the juggling of changes. The main difficulty with technology is that someone may find themselves locked out of access to file while someone else is reviewing a document.

Revising the Manuscript

Again, project managers must avoid pride of ownership regarding drafts. They need to consider suggestions with an open mind, which is easier said than done. The best approach is to first view suggestions from the reader's perspective and then give the benefit of doubt to the suggestions.

Revisions will come in three levels. The first is to look at grammar. Just as important, however, project managers must look at the content, specifically paying attention to logical flow and the detail support for an idea. They also must look at the layout of content to determine whether it enhances or retards readability and comprehension.

Project managers might find it valuable to retain revisions for a time. Retention serves two purposes. One, it provides an effective audit trail for reconstructing the history of revisions. Second, a revision, particularly for content, may provide additional direction or information to develop future documentation. Of course, project managers are the ultimate judge for the quality of documentation on their projects.

Receiving Approval or Disapproval

The same approaches to conduct reviews apply for obtaining approvals: sequential, concurrent, or group. The advantages and disadvantages are the same, too. Project managers might consider keeping a timeline. For example, project managers might use the record to protect themselves from accusations of preparing the documentation arbitrarily or not consulting the right stakeholders.

After receiving all the necessary approvals, place a document under configuration control. No one can alter it whimsically. Proposed changes by readers or project managers must go through an impact analysis to determine whether a change can occur. Project managers or someone with configuration management responsibilities might be the ones who maintain the configuration. Regardless, project managers must make special effort to maintain the integrity of a document after receiving the necessary approvals.

Publishing or Distributing the Document

Project managers can now release a document to readers. This task was once laborious. However, thanks to information technology, distributing a new document has become easier. Project managers can create very specific distribution lists for a select readership. They can also store documents in a repository or on a Web site.

A major challenge is ensuring people use the most recent version of a document. It can prove quite useful to add on a front page of a document stating that only the online version is an authorized version. This caveat will encourage readers to visit the Web site to read the most recent version.

Maintaining and Updating Documents

Circumstances may warrant changing documentation by adding, deleting, or modifying content. Project managers follow the same approaches to revise, approve, and publish a document.

Changes may come via an ad hoc request. Depending on magnitude, project managers may elect to "batch" changes and then send the document for review and approval. Another option is for project managers to set a schedule for periodic reviews of documentation with select readers and then publish the updated document at certain prescribed dates, or block points.

Different Types of Supporting Material

Regardless of the type of documentation, the content will likely involve one or more of these items: text, graphics, diagrams, and tables. What follows are a few heuristics to follow regarding these items.

Charts and diagrams. All should have a unique designator, such as "Figure 1.1," and a descriptive title. They should also contain only content that communicates a specific message. Too much clutter in a chart adds to confusion and makes a message incomprehensible. Charts (bar charts, too) should have a legend, especially if they contain several icons. The print must be large enough to read content. Finally, text should reference charts and diagrams. Just having a chart on a page with no reference in text gives the impression that the project manager may only be interested in filling space. If a document has a large number of charts and diagrams, consider compiling a list of illustrations at the beginning of the text.

Tables. Like charts and diagrams, tables should have a unique designator and a descriptive title, perhaps a caption. They should only contain the content that communicates a message. If project managers present a table with too much content readers may become confused, which will hinder their comprehension. Project managers who fail to simplify their messages will make work for themselves by having to give subsequent explanations or correct misunderstanding. If project managers must present substantial detail, they might consider summarizing content (e.g., rounding numbers, if possible, or highlighting content to illustrate a point). If

Subject: QUALITY

No. 8

References: ISO 9000

Supersedes: Policy 8, June 11, 1988

Owner: Project Manager

Date: January 20, 2020

Quality is one of the company's top priorities, especially if it expects to sustain its prominence in the industry. Therefore, this project will follow all requirements of ISO 9000 in all its activities. Any exceptions to this policy must receive the approval of the steering committee.

[signed]
Project Manager

Figure 6.3   Example of a policy.

content has a large number of tables, project managers might compile a list of tables at the beginning of a document.

Common Types of Documentation

Projects use all types of documentation. The most common documents are procedures, reports, checklists, forms, matrices, flowcharts, glossaries, and charts (Figure 6.3).

Procedures. These documents cover the administrative and the technical aspects of managing a project. All procedures should contain (besides the text and graphics) a title, unique designator, effective date, date-time stamp, pagination, and references. The content should provide the basics for answering the who, what, when, where, why, and hows of a topic in an outline format.

There are basically four types of procedures: step-by-step, item-by-item, narrative, and playscript.

A step-by-step format describes sequential or linear activities, such as submitting schedule status in an automated tool. A playscript format describes sequential and linear activities involving more than one person in the execution. An item-by-item format describes nonsequential activity or information, such as managing different types of information on a project.

A narrative format describes any topic. This format often leads to wordiness and makes it difficult for the reader to find information. A heuristic for using a narrative format is when one person executes content involving five or less steps.

SUBMITTING STATUS USING REPORTING SOFTWARE

All designated leads for each of the work packages for this project must update status every Thursday by 3 p.m., Eastern Time. Each lead will enter actual and remaining hours for each task as well as applicable start and completion dates. Note: if for some reason status is unable to meet the 3 p.m. time, the lead must notify the project manager via phone and an estimated time when the status will be submitted.

I. COLLECT STATUS
    a. Collect status from each of the people working on the relevant tasks for each of the work packages. This status should include, if applicable, this data for each task:
        i. Actual hours
        ii. Estimated remaining hours or expected completion date
        iii. Actual start date
        iv. Actual finish date
    Note: This status should be from the day after of the previous data date.
    b. Verify that the data collected is consistent from the previous weeks.

II. ENTER DATA ONLINE
    a. Sign into the Project Management Portal.
    b. Click on the status software icon in the upper right.
    c. Select the name of the project from the pull down list.
    d. Type in you user identification and password.
    e. Note: The tasks for you to status will appear.
    f. Enter the data for the applicable tasks.

III. SUBMIT DATA
    a. Click on the submit button

Note: Your data will automatically be submitted to the project's data base.

Figure 6.4   Example of project procedure written in step-by-step format.

Forms. The basic purposes of forms are to capture information and provide an audit trail. Good forms provide clear and concise instructions, capture only the necessary data, and have a unique designator (e.g., number, source, destination, and title). The source and destination of a form are captured in the instructions.

Two problems exist with forms. People often create too many of them, and they frequently capture more data than is necessary. When the volume in number of forms and amount of content gets too big, people reluctantly complete the documents. Or even worse, they give up and stop completing the documents, leading to a loss of data. Fortunately, automated tools provide an effective way to develop more focused, online forms which, in turn, can populate a repository. A number of data base tools are available to develop online forms. After people complete the fields, the data are loaded in a spreadsheet or some other application. The captured data can then be combined with other data to produce reports, either in graphical or tabular form.

SCHEDULE BASELINE

At no time should a deviation from the logic of the schedule should occur unless formally approved by the change board. All requests should occur at least one week in advance and should be submitted to the project manager for preliminary review. All requests can be submitted by e-mail or through the completion of the Change Request Form. If the request is submitted via e-mail, the contents of the message must cover all the fields in the Change Request Form; the submitter can also complete the form and attach it to an e-mail.

I.   INITIATE REQUEST

    Requestor   1. Obtain change request form.

                                    2. **Complete change request form.**

                                    3. Make photocopy of request for records.

                                    4. Send original to project manager.

    Project Manager   5. Review form for completeness.

                                        a. If request requires additional information, return form to requestor for additional information.

                                        b. If request is complete, sign and date the form.

                                    6. Submit the form to the configuration management specialist.

    Configuration Management
    Specialist   7. Record the date having received the form.

                                      8. **Sign the form.**

                                    9. Contact the requestor and project manager to inform them of receiving the form and when it will be considered by the change board.

II.   PROCESS REQUEST

    Configuration Management
    Specialist   10. Submit change request to change board.

    Change Board   11. Determine the following for the request:
                                        - Priority (high, medium, low)
                                        - Impact (high, medium, low)
                                        - Impact to cost, schedule, and quality
                                        - Approve or disapprove
                                        - Implementation

    Configuration Management
    Specialist   12. Notify requestor of decision by change board.

Figure 6.5   **Example of project procedure written in playscript format.**

RESPONDING TO INQUIRIES FROM POTENTIAL CONTRACTORS

Inquiries from potential contractors can come from many places. They can come from attending conferences or a random call. It is the policy of our company that you direct any inquiries to our procurement organization to preclude any potential conflict of interest. While you may find that a contractor has a good idea or offers a product at a competitive price substantially different from a current supplier, no one on the project is authorized to negotiate or compromise anything on behalf of the company.

If anyone violates this procedure, they could be subject to disciplinary action or even face termination from employment.

Figure 6.6 Example of project procedure written in narrative format.

Checklists. These documents share many of the characteristics of forms (e.g., instructions, title, unique designator). The most common purpose is to ensure that team members complete specific tasks. Project managers use checklists also to help people submit their status or to develop a realistic schedule. For example, project managers might provide a checklist to help people on a team to remember what specific data to enter into a scheduling tool. The checklist might include actual start, actual finish, percent complete, actual hours, remaining hours, etc.

Flowcharts. Project management involves myriad flowcharts. Most of the flowcharting types depend on the flow of control. With the advent of information systems thinking, however, other flowchart types (e.g., data, process, and object based) appear more frequently. In some cases, flowcharts look more like road maps that employ clipart to reflect strategy or the interaction of people, organizations, and things (e.g., computing technology).

Whatever the format, project managers should consider these guidelines: have a title, provide a legend for the symbols used, and be referenced in the text.

Flowcharts and road maps face a major challenge when incorporated in a document: clarity. Too often, flowcharts and road maps contain too many symbols, making comprehension very difficult. A good heuristic to deal with this situation is to ensure that the first flowchart or road map is at a high enough level of abstraction which can, in turn, then explode each symbol into finer detail as a separate diagram. For example, some project managers like to draw data flow diagrams. A data flow diagram, or DFD, consists of a series of bubbles representing processes. Each bubble can be exploded into more discrete sets of functions, or bubbles. The deeper the explosion of a bubble into more finite ones, the more specific subfunctions are identified until explosion no longer seems necessary.

Matrices. These documents effectively display data and information under different conditions. What a project manager might ordinarily, for example, display in a lengthy flowchart can be shown in a matrix. This information may be linear or non-linear data or information used under various conditions or circumstances.

A matrix consists of cells that contain a specific value or range of values. The leftmost column reflects various components, items, or actions. The topmost row reflects the different attributes or conditions that may exist. A cell represents the intersection between a specific condition and an attribute. The content of a cell reflects the desired value resulting between the left column and top row. A matrix is an excellent way to display a large number of values in a compact way. A matrix is also useful to see the impact of a specific attribute or condition on a variable.

A matrix incorporated in a document should have a title, and the contents of each cell should be clear and concise. Avoid the temptation to cram each cell with too much material for one simple reason: too large a matrix can be impossible to print on a single sheet of paper. Like flowcharts, if a matrix becomes too large, consider exploding each cell into further detail, such as into another matrix.

Glossary. Project managers might consider developing a glossary for highly technical documents. A glossary serves several purposes, perhaps the most important as providing a way to avoid confusion over terminology. For example, even from a project management perspective, "critical path" can have different meanings to people. To a project manager, it means the longest path in the network diagram but to an engineer something else—an important component being built, regardless of time.

When developing a glossary, consider two important guidelines. First, avoid using the same word in the description. Second, use only words residing in the contents of a document. Remember that project managers are creating a glossary, not a dictionary.

Reports. Of all the documentation produced on a project, the most common, and perhaps most important, are reports. Project managers produce reports about cost, schedule, and quality performance. These reports take the form of tables, graphics, or narrative text.

A number of guidelines exist to consider when developing reports, regardless of format.

The first guideline is to tailor all reports to the needs of the readers. Management tends to require higher-level reports consisting of summary information that shows current status and projections into the future. The customer often requires the same level but at a greater level of detail. The team requires reports containing a high level of detail, frequently related to their own performance relative to that of the overall project.

Another guideline is to ensure that each report has all the characteristics of other documentation. For example, a report should have a title and a date time stamp. It may also contain instructions on interpreting content.

A final guideline is to archive reports from one generation to next. Through archiving, project managers will maintain an audit trail of a project's performance. This audit trail can help in not only developing lessons learned but also satisfying the needs of auditors. Archiving of reports can assist in performing postimplementation reviews of projects. After a few months following the delivery of a product or service, auditors can use the reports to reconstruct the past to ascertain how the state of a product or service exists the way it does today.

The Project Manual

Project managers can assemble all project documentation into a project manual. This manual can contain just about anything deemed relevant to a project, including contact lists, procedures, reports, forms, and flowcharts.

A project manual offers three principal advantages. One advantage is that it conveniently allows for stakeholders to access pertinent documentation. Another advantage is that it serves as an excellent tool to get new project participants up to speed about a project. Finally, it saves stakeholders time in searching for a particular document.

For a project manual to prove useful to its recipients, follow these guidelines.

1. The manual must have a title and table of contents. The table of contents should match content, not an easy task if the documentation constantly changes due to updates to material.
2. It should be accessible to the people needing the materials. In the past accessibility was a problem. With the advent of information technology people can gain access, however, to a Web site or a server; that is, if they have an online connection.
3. Even if a manual is online, project managers must consider a host of administrative considerations. Everyone who needs access must have the capability to do so and have the appropriate security passes to access certain data and information. Cost considerations for having an online manual might include effort and money. These considerations might include providing people with the tools and storage.
4. Project managers must address maintenance considerations, such as updates and new material. These considerations need to determine reviews and approvals for materials and the frequency of updates.
5. Legal considerations are very important. Any material in a document cannot violate copyright. Also, certain information may require restricted access either because it is proprietary or deals with intellectual capital. Therefore, specific controls must exist to preclude unauthorized access to such materials. On projects that involve external partners, controlling this type of access may be necessary.

Typical contents of a project manual might include:

- Agendas
- Bar (Gantt) charts
- Charters
- Contact listings
- Forms
- Matrices
- Organization charts

- Policies
- Procedures
- Reports
- Resource list
- Roles, responsibilities, and authorities
- Schedules (network)
- Statement of work
- Work breakdown structure
- Workflows

The Right Amount

Documentation can be a project's best friend and its worst enemy. Too much or little data and information can cause communications problems. Too much documentation gives importance to data and information that might not deserve it. Too little documentation presents the misfortune of overlooking very important data and information. The key is to find the right amount of documentation that enables progress rather than regression. The best approach is to know who will use the documentation and their expectations of it on a project.

Getting Started Checklist		
Question	*Yes*	*No*
1. When preparing a document for a project, do you perform these activities:		
Define readers?		
Determine their goals?		
Conduct research?		
Prepare an outline?		
Create a document?		
Conduct the review?		
Revise the manuscript?		
Seek approval/disapproval?		
Publish and distribute the document?		
Maintain and update the document?		
2. When conducting interviews, do you:		
Prepare in advance?		

Getting Started Checklist (Continued)		
Question	*Yes*	*No*
	Determine the type of questions to ask?		
	Conduct the interview away from the interviewee's locus of activity, if possible?		
	Focus on the purpose of the interview?		
	Provide the interviewee with some idea of the type of questions to ask?		
	Apply effective and active listening skills during the interview?		
3.	Is your documentation:		
	A combination of analysis and synthesis?		
	Complete without overkill?		
	Direct and to the point?		
	Objective?		
	Specific in the choice of language?		
	Written clearly?		
4.	Does each policy or procedure have:		
	An introduction?		
	Discussion section?		
	Conclusion?		
5.	Does the discussion section of each document have one of these formats:		
	Chronology?		
	Comparison and contrast?		
	Conditional?		
	Definitions?		
	Issues, facts, and conclusions?		
	Problem–solution?		
	Process description?		
	Spatial arrangement?		
	Stakeholder or customer?		
	Topical?		
6.	When preparing documentation, do you consider these style points:		
	Clarity?		
	Conciseness?		
	Constructiveness?		

Getting Started Checklist (Continued)		
Question	*Yes*	*No*
Appropriateness?		
7. When conducting reviews, do you use:		
Concurrent reviews?		
Group reviews?		
Serial reviews?		
8. For supporting material for documentation do you use:		
Charts?		
Diagrams?		
Tables?		
9. Do you consider the different types of documentation to develop, such as:		
Checklists?		
Flowcharts?		
Forms?		
Glossary?		
Matrices?		
Procedures:		
Step-by-step?		
Item-by-item?		
Narrative?		
Playscript?		
Reports?		
10. If preparing a project manual, do you consider including these topics:		
Agendas		
Bar (Gantt) charts		
Charter		
Contact listings		
Forms		
Matrices		
Organization charts		
Policies		
Procedures		
Reports		

Getting Started Checklist (Continued)		
Question	*Yes*	*No*
Resource list		
Roles, responsibilities, and authorities		
Schedules (network)		
Statement of work		
Work breakdown structure		
Work flows		

Chapter 7

Conducting Meetings

A meeting is one of the most effective communications tools for project managers. Unfortunately, many project managers fail to effectively use meetings to further the interests of their projects. Instead, their meetings become counterproductive, hindering rather than furthering productivity.

PMIS Contributions

A PMIS can help project managers to manage meetings in several ways. It can provide source material for topics of discussion. It can store results of previous meetings which can be reviewed at a later meeting. If automated, it can allow participants to access text, tables, and graphics in real-time to clarify a point or make a decision. It also provides an excellent means for following up on decisions made at previous meetings.

Reasons for Meetings

Project managers have meetings for many reasons. These reasons include:

- Answering questions or clarifying issues on cost, schedule, and quality
- Collecting and reviewing status
- Collecting or sharing information
- Developing and reviewing different elements of a project plan
- Kicking off a project

■ Making key decisions at critical points in the life cycle, for example, at the beginning or end of a phase or project
■ Managing changes
■ Solving a technical or business management problem or issue

An important point is warranted. Project managers should not set up meetings simply for the sake of having a meeting. They should have them only when necessary and for the minimum time required. Of course, much depends on the corporate culture, but too many meetings may indicate a dysfunctional situation. Meetings must occur sparingly and meaningfully if they are to contribute to the successful outcomes of projects.

Reasons for Meeting Failure

Unfortunately, meetings often go awry because of a failure to:

■ Agree upon and communicate expectations
■ Apply effective listening skills
■ Assign roles and responsibilities
■ Document results
■ Encourage participation
■ Establish and maintain structure
■ Follow up on outstanding issues and actions
■ Give people equal opportunity and time to speak
■ Identify the appropriate attendees
■ Inform people in advance about the meeting
■ Keep within a specified timeframe
■ Resolve conflict effectively
■ Set objectives
■ Share information and raise important questions

The bottom line is that meetings in a project environment fail for many reasons. However, the three primary ones are lack of focus, unavailability of key people, and no follow-through on actions. Project managers are often the initiators and architects of meetings and, therefore, must work hard to preclude any of the aforementioned reasons for failure to occur.

Indicators of Poor Meetings

Not surprisingly, people find meetings more of a liability than an asset. Some indicators of poorly planned and executed meetings include:

- Conflicts surface and resurface
- Lack of consistent or poor attendance
- Lack of focus
- Lack of rapport among attendees
- No follow-up on results
- No one listening
- No one sticking to the agenda
- No results from the meeting
- No visibility of results
- People coming unprepared
- People making constant excuses for not attending
- People not participating or sharing information
- Starting or finishing late

Key Steps for Successful Meetings

Regardless of the type of meeting, more effective ones are possible by performing simple yet essential actions: planning the meeting; conducting it; and following up on results (Figure 7.1).

Planning the Meeting

By planning meetings, project managers will have a much easier time conducting them and following up on results. If they fail to plan or treat meetings as ad hoc occurrences, however, they will fail to meet objectives.

To have effective meetings, therefore, consider these guidelines:

- Determine:
    - Attendees/invitees
    - Frequency of occurrence
    - Goals and objectives
    - Location
    - Place
    - Purpose

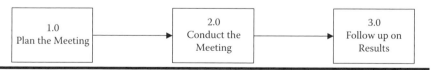

Figure 7.1   Meetings flowchart.

```
     I.    Purpose
     II.   Goals and Objectives of the Meeting
     III.  Background
     IV.   Gate Criteria
     V.    Performance
           A. Cost
           B. Metrics
           C. To Date
     VI.   Estimate-at-Completion
           A. Schedule
           B. Metrics
           C. To Date
     VII.  Estimate-at-Completion
     VIII. Quality
           A. Metrics
           B. To Date
           C. Estimate-at-Completion
     IX.   Go/No-Go Decision
     X.    Look Ahead
     XI.   Help Needed
     XII.  Next Step
```

Figure 7.2   Agenda for a checkpoint (gate) review.

```
     I.     Introduction of new people

     II.    Important news

     III.   Administrative considerations

     IV.    Technical considerations

     V.     Information sharing

     VI.    Round robin
```

Figure 7.3   Agenda for a project staff meeting.

- – Sufficient advance notification
- – Supplies and equipment
- – Time and length of time
- ■ Prepare an agenda (Figures 7.2–7.6).
- ■ Visit the location ahead of time.
- ■ Identify all desired roles and responsibilities (facilitator, recorder, etc.).

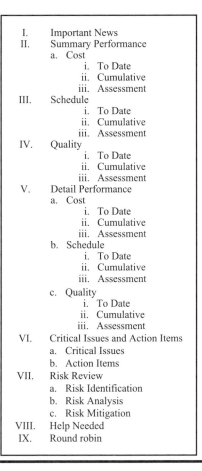

I.   Important News
II.   Summary Performance
        a. Cost
                i.   To Date
                ii. Cumulative
                iii. Assessment
III.   Schedule
                i.   To Date
                ii. Cumulative
                iii. Assessment
IV.   Quality
                i.   To Date
                ii. Cumulative
                iii. Assessment
V.   Detail Performance
        a. Cost
                i.   To Date
                ii. Cumulative
                iii. Assessment
        b. Schedule
                i.   To Date
                ii. Cumulative
                iii. Assessment
        c. Quality
                i.   To Date
                ii. Cumulative
                iii. Assessment
VI.   Critical Issues and Action Items
        a. Critical Issues
        b. Action Items
VII.   Risk Review
        a. Risk Identification
        b. Risk Analysis
        c. Risk Mitigation
VIII.   Help Needed
IX.   Round robin

Figure 7.4   Agenda for a status review meeting.

Conducting the Meeting

The actual occurrence of a meeting can test even the most able project manager. Despite challenges, a well-conducted meeting can have spectacular project results. Meetings that are defined, planned, organized, executed, and controlled—just like any project—can become project managers' tools for conducting projects efficiently and effectively. A successful meeting on a project can help develop ways to deal with cost and schedule problems and obstacles or a seemingly insurmountable technical issue. Successful project managers accomplish that by getting the involvement of stakeholders at these meetings.

```
    I.      Minutes from previous meeting
            a. Revisions
            b. Approval/Disapproval
    II.     Log of change requests
            a. Open
            b. Closed
            c. Suspended
    III.    Review log for open change requests
    IV.     Assessment of each open change request
            a. Priority (high, medium, low)
            b. Impact
                    i. Cost (high, medium, low)
                   ii. Schedule (high, medium, low)
                  iii. Quality (high, medium, low)
    V.      Disposition of request
            a. Approve
            b. Disapprove
            c. Suspend

    VI.     Block point (implementation date) for each approved change request
    VII.    Round robin
```

Figure 7.5   Agenda for a change board meeting.

```
    I.      Issues
            a. Open issues since previous meeting
                    i. Total Number
                   ii. Description
            b. Closed issues from previous meeting
                    i. Total Number
                   ii. Description
            c. Open issues to address today
                    i. Total Number
                   ii. Description
            d. Remaining open issues
                    i. Total Number
                   ii. Description
    II.     Information sharing
    III.    Help Needed
    IV.     Round robin
```

Figure 7.6   Agenda for a daily standup meeting.

However, conducting a meeting doesn't just happen. Project managers must be alert enough to effectively perform these suggested guidelines:

- Agree on rules for decision making, if applicable.
- Apply active and effective listening skills.
- Break frequently—on the hour, for example.
- Conduct a periodic process check.
- Encourage open sharing of ideas and information.
- Ensure everyone understands their roles and responsibilities.
- Establish a parking lot for stray ideas or comments to consider, if time permits or at a later meeting.
- Follow the agenda.
- Have sufficient backups for equipment and supplies.
- Keep the meeting free from distractions (noise, irrelevant comments, etc.).
- Provide everyone with an opportunity to participate.
- Record results.
- Reiterate the purpose, goals, and objectives.
- Seek win–win results concerning solutions to problems.
- Stress the need for empathy and diversity.
- Use positive conflict management.

Follow up on Results

Project managers' roles and responsibilities should not end after the conduct of a meeting. In fact, to ensure that the meeting achieves its purpose, goals, and objectives, they should perform these suggested guidelines:

- Be available to clarify contents of the meeting record and to maintain an open dialogue with attendees.
- Determine the medium to distribute the results.
- Distribute the record of the meeting (e.g., minutes, presentations) in a timely and accessible way.
- If necessary, schedule a follow-up meeting or remind attendees of the next regularly scheduled one.
- Periodically remind people of their responsibilities for following up on assigned tasks or action items.

Holding Effective Virtual Meetings

Information technology has made it possible for project team members to be spread across a continent and never meet with one another. Virtual team meetings are becoming the norm in many companies as more employees find themselves working at home, far away from the home office, or traveling frequently.

There are plenty of benefits and challenges with virtual meetings. The benefits often relate to efficiency; the challenges relate to effectiveness.

Virtual meetings can save time and money. The cost of travel and the time to get to a destination are dramatically reduced. People can participate in a comfortable location.

The challenges of virtual meetings are frequently overshadowed by the efficiencies. These challenges include the difficulty in assessing whether the listener is really engaged in a conversation; the inability to view and interpret body language; inability to adapt to situations when the technology fails to operate; and failure of some attendees to attend.

To increase the effectiveness of virtual team meetings, project managers should consider these guidelines:

- Check the equipment for operability before the meeting starts.
- Ensure the e-mail notification of the meeting has the call-in number, an agenda, and a copy of any presentations.
- Finish the meeting with a recap and do a round-robin by asking each person if he or she has anything to say.
- For key decisions, either ask if anyone objects or poll each person.
- Give everyone an opportunity to speak.
- Have everyone introduce themselves before conducting business.
- Have people say their name before they speak (especially for a large number of attendees).
- Keep track of time.
- Provide an agenda.
- Start and finish on time.

Passing through the Impasse

Sometimes meetings reach what appears to be an impasse. Many of the attendees either cannot see another person's point of view or they do not want to consider an alternate viewpoint. Either way, the meeting fails to move forward and, consequently, nothing results from the meeting other than a large sense of frustration.

Many times, however, an impasse is not because of anything intentional. Rather, it is because people see reality differently. That is, their paradigms or mental models are so different that they are unable to see another viewpoint.

A paradigm is essentially a model of perceiving and interpreting how the world works. It is based upon a set of assumptions, beliefs, values, and rules that provide a framework that allows people to adapt to the world. Many times these paradigms are so strong that they actually make adaptation to the world more difficult rather than easier, especially if the world around them is changing. This change can cause people to alter the elements of their paradigm or cause them to do just the opposite, such as becoming inflexible as a reaction to anything that challenges the fundamental beliefs and values. When this circumstance happens, communications frequently breaks down and an impasse occurs until something dramatically forces change. Then a paradigm shift occurs because the problems cannot be dealt with by the prevailing paradigm.

Paradigm shifts are quite difficult to achieve on projects, especially on technical ones. The reason is that people come from different disciplines each with its unique perspective on completing a set of tasks or even an entire project. Project managers have to work hard to encourage people to become more flexible in thinking and applying their skills. However, not just technical projects have this problem. Projects involving people from multiple business units may experience the same phenomena, whereby each unit has a different perspective on how to go about managing a project.

It is very difficult, of course, for people to step outside of their paradigm in order to consider a different point of view. At meetings, this circumstance is an especially frequent reality. A controversial idea arises, the polarization among viewpoints can easily surface, and then progress can halt.

Edward de Bono, however, has provided a technique for overcoming stalemates that often occur at meetings. He developed the concept of thinking hats that are identified with different colors (Figure 7.7). Each hat represents a pattern of thinking and can be worn by participants to help remove them from a mental rut.

Red Hat thinking deals with using emotion to address issues, problems, and concerns. Hunches, intuition, and feelings play important roles. Red Hat thinkers rely on subjectivity and make choices based on values. An example is project managers who place less emphasis on facts and data and more on decisions using gut feelings.

Thinking Hat Pattern	*Characteristics*
Red Hat	• Uses emotions to deal with issues, problems, and concerns • Subjective and choices based on value
White Hat	• Emphasizes facts and data • Stresses objectivity and independence
Yellow Hat	• Emphasizes the positive • Looks at benefits and takes a constructive approach
Black Hat	• Emphasizes the negative • Looks at the reason's against something
Green Hat	• Looks outside the box • Considers different alternatives
Blue Hat	• Emphasizes organization and content • Places importance on discipline and logical sequence

Figure 7.7 Thinking hats summary table.

White Hat thinking is just the opposite of Red Hat thinking. This thinking places importance on facts and data, especially in a manner that emphasizes objectivity and independence. An example is project managers who emphasize facts and data (e.g., schedule performance index (SPI) over subjective factors like intuition).

Yellow Hat thinking sees the world as "half full." This thinking emphasizes the positive aspects of something. This thinking requires looking at benefits and taking a constructive approach for dealing with issues and problems. An example is project managers who can turn a problem or obstacle into "lemonade." They focus on what can be done with the circumstances dealt to the project to deliver a positive result.

Black Hat thinking views the world as "half empty." This thinking looks for all the reasons against something. This thinking places importance on negative logic with an orientation towards pessimism. Often, these thinkers will identify risks and have no problem pointing out erroneous thinking. An example is project managers who can identify the shortcomings of an idea or approach and ensure that some type of mitigation or contingency plan is in place.

Green Hat thinking requires looking at the issues and problems as a means for thinking outside the box. This thinking requires looking at different alternatives to deal with issues and problems. This thinking style places importance on developing creative and innovative approaches for dealing with issues and problems. An example is project managers who like to brainstorm or explore options for overcoming problems or obstacles. They will likely employ "blue sky" techniques to develop innovative, even revolutionary solutions.

Blue Hat thinking is the cop of the six hats. This thinking emphasizes organization and control after defining exactly what the issue or problem really is. More so than other thinking styles, this one places importance on discipline and logical sequence. An example is project managers who view themselves as protectors of their projects. While not inflexible, they often will question the wisdom behind a new idea or approach. The key is having their stamp of approval before anyone can proceed.

According to de Bono no one thinking style is better or worse than any other. In fact, each person, to varying degrees, can wear each of the hats. By wearing the appropriate hat at a given time, either on an individual or group basis, meetings can progress more smoothly and have a greater opportunity to achieve their intended purposes.

Successful project managers have the ability to determine which hat they or any stakeholder should wear under a specific circumstance. Any hat they choose is not contingent upon the project phase but the circumstances surrounding an issue or obstacle.

Dealing with "Bad Eggs"

In any group endeavor, and especially meetings, an impasse can occur for reasons other than thinking styles. A major reason is because of difficult people. When one or more difficult people are present who exhibit a negative pattern of behavior, this can sour the entire atmosphere of a meeting and nothing seems to get done. Like thinking styles, a number of different types of difficult people exist (Figure 7.8).

Author Robert Bramson has identified several patterns of behavior exhibited by difficult people. Every project manager should have a good understanding of his work because Bramson provides a good insight on dealing with a variety of types of difficult people. Failure to deal with difficult people at meetings often results in ones that achieve nothing; it also creates an atmosphere of negativism that languishes long after the conclusion of these sessions.

Bramson identifies several patterns of difficult people.

Hostile-Aggressives are just what the name implies. They are the people who are pushy and like to use intimidation to have their way. They tend to be arbitrary and arrogant when dealing with people. An example is a stakeholder at a status review meeting who tries to pull people away from the agenda and talk about a topic that interests him or her.

Complainers are the people who are never satisfied. They continually gripe about everything while simultaneously never offering a solution. Although there may be some truth to their complaints, they seldom take action to change the circumstances that would alleviate their complaints. An example is a stakeholder at an ad hoc meeting who constantly complains about a tool (e.g., software) but offers no alternative.

Pattern of Behavior	*Characteristics*
Hostile Aggressive	• Pushy and uses intimidation • Arbitrary and arrogant
Complainer	• Gripe without offering a solution • Seldom takes action to rectify a situation
Silent and Non-Responsive	• Not very communicative • Relies on others to share their feelings and thoughts
Super-Agreeable	• Never commit themselves • Fears rejection
Negativist	• Are fatalists • Often nay sayers
Know-It-All	• Self-appointed expert • Condescending
Indecisive	• Delays making decisions • Fear of hurting or alienating someone

Figure 7.8   Difficult people summary table.

Silent and Non-Responsives are people with few words yet they are difficult to deal with because they never open up. Instead, they require continual effort expended by others to get them to share their feelings and thoughts. If they do manage to open up they do so reluctantly and in a guarded way. Stakeholders who sit at a team meeting and never speak up unless pushed to the point of doing so are an example. Even then, they speak cryptically.

Super-Agreeables are everyone's pal who never really commit to anything or produce anything that will result in controversy. Because they fear rejection they will commit to something even though they know that they can never deliver. Stakeholders who will commit to just about everything in a work-breakdown, structure-development session and never follow through on tasks are an example. If they do, the deliverables are marginal at best.

Negativists are people who say words like "impossible" or "it will never work." They are the fatalists who believe that whatever thought or action taken will have less than favorable results. They are nay sayers. Stakeholders who shoot down any new idea or approach that doesn't meet their undisclosed standards at a working session to solve a problem are an example. Ironically, they are the same people who offer no solutions.

Know-It-Alls are often experts who come across as the paragons of logic who strive to impress and even put people down in a very condescending way. Chances are they are the only people who listen to themselves. Stakeholders who constantly speak on any topic at project team meetings and do so without listening to other people are an example. They expound on an idea for what seems like eons without even taking the hint from others that it is time to yield the floor.

Indecisives are the people who cannot make a decision or delay making one until they have no other choice. At the extreme, they may even allow someone to make a decision for them. Often, they will not make a decision for fear of hurting or alienating someone. This indecisiveness is reflected in deflection and indirectness. Stakeholders, like some project managers, who cannot make a critical decision at a status review meeting or at a working team meeting are an example. Typically, these people need more data and information (which is never enough) before making a decision.

To add complexity to dealing with difficult people, Bramson notes that there are varieties of the patterns of difficult people. Fortunately, project managers do not have to feel totally overwhelmed by these patterns of behavior. He suggests these coping skills, which he defines as actions to minimize the impact of these behaviors: (1) determine whether or not a person is exhibiting the behavior of a difficult person, (2) stop hoping to change the difficult person, (3) keep both mental and physical distance, (4) develop a plan of attack for dealing with the relationship, (5) implement the plan, and (6) monitor and adjust accordingly.

Rules for Meetings

One of the biggest trends in corporations is putting posters on the walls of conference rooms that provide a checklist of behaviors and activities that should occur at meetings. These posters include guidelines related to civility like:

- Avoid shouting or use of abusive language.
- Clean the room before departing.
- Concentrate on the problem or issue, not personality differences.
- Focus on the meeting's purpose.
- Give everyone a chance to speak.
- Respect other people's point of view or opinion.
- Stop all side conversations.
- Turn off devices like cell phones and personal computers.
- Use effective and active listening.

These posters really are nothing more than reminders to people about the importance of respecting each other. Sometimes during the heat of a meeting some people lose their sense of civility, and the posters are a reminder that decorum should be the rule rather than the exception.

In some cases, rooms may lack these posters. Project managers might find it useful, therefore, to develop and display a slide of their own to help ensure that meetings begin and end with civility. They might also give attendees the opportunity to add or revise items on the slide.

Worst and Best of Times

Meetings can be the most productive tool of project managers. Unfortunately, many project managers fail to manage the use of this tool very effectively. Sometimes, team members and other stakeholders find themselves wanting to avoid meetings like the plague. Project managers can have the same feelings. Yet, most of what a project manager does cannot happen without meetings. It is incumbent upon project managers to ensure that their meetings occur both efficiently and effectively so that the sessions make the best use of their own time and that of attendees.

Getting Started Checklist		
Question	Yes	No
1. Have you determined whether to have any of these categories of meetings?		
Checkpoint Review		
Project Staff		
Status Review		
Change Board		
2. When planning a meeting do you follow to these guidelines?		
Determine:		
Attendees/invitees		
Frequency of occurrence		
Goals and objectives		
Location		
Place		
Purpose		
Sufficient advance notification		
Supplies and equipment		
Time and length of time		
Identify all desired roles and responsibilities (e.g., facilitator, recorder)		
Prepare an agenda		
Visit the location ahead of time		
3. When planning a meeting do you follow to these guidelines?		
Agree on rules for decision making, if applicable.		
Apply active and effective listening skills.		
Break frequently, e.g., on the hour.		
Conduct a periodic process check.		
Encourage open sharing of ideas and information.		
Ensure everyone understands their roles and responsibilities.		
Establish a parking lot for stray ideas or comments to consider, if time permitted or at a later meeting.		
Follow the agenda.		
Have sufficient backups for equipment and supplies.		

Getting Started Checklist (Continued)		
Question	*Yes*	*No*
Keep the meeting free from distractions (e.g., noise, irrelevant comments).		
Provide everyone with an opportunity to participate.		
Record results.		
4. After each meeting, do you follow these guidelines?		
Be available to clarify contents of the meeting record and to maintain an open dialogue with attendees.		
Determine the medium to distribute the results.		
Distribute the record of the meeting (e.g., minutes, presentations) in a timely and accessible way.		
If necessary, schedule a follow-up meeting or remind them of the next regularly scheduled one.		
5. When conducting a meeting, do you use any of these Thinking Hats?		
Black Hat		
Blue Hat		
Green Hat		
Red Hat		
White Hat		
Yellow Hat		
6. During meetings have you thought about who are the following types of difficult people and given some thought on how to deal with them?		
Complainers		
Hostile-Aggressives		
Indecisiveness		
Know-It-Alls		
Negativists		
Silent and Non-Responsives		
Super-Agreeables		
7. Do you consider any of these rules for meetings?		
Avoid shouting or use of abusive language.		
Clean the room before departing.		

Getting Started Checklist (Continued)		
Question	*Yes*	*No*
Concentrate on the problem or issue, not personality differences.		
Focus on the meeting's purpose.		
Give everyone a chance to speak.		
Respect other people's point of view or opinion.		
Stop all side conversations.		
Turn off devices like cell phones and personal computers.		
Use effective and active listening.		
8. When conducting virtual meetings, do you consider these guidelines?		
Check the equipment for operability before the meeting starts.		
Ensure the e-mail notification of the meeting has the call-in number, an agenda, and a copy of any presentations.		
Finish the meeting with a recap and do a round robin by asking each person if he or she has anything to say.		
For key decisions, either ask if anyone objects or poll each person.		
Give everyone an opportunity to speak.		
Have everyone introduce themselves before conducting business.		
Have people say their name before they speak (especially for a large number of attendees).		
Keep track of time.		
Provide an agenda.		
Start and finish on time.		

Chapter 8

Giving Effective Presentations

Having the ability and expertise to present effectively is one of the most critical skills project managers can have. When considering the roles that project managers play, it is easy to appreciate the importance of communicating. Project managers are the "linchpins," interacting with a large, diversified group of people, requiring them to present effectively and regularly.

PMIS Contributions

As with documentation, a PMIS can make considerable contributions. For one, it can provide a great wealth of source material for a presentation. For another, it can provide material to buttress significant points in a pitch by allowing project managers to pull up real-time information to make a point. Finally, it can help project managers to pull applicable data from a repository to investigate or counter any disagreements that may arise on the spot.

Many Opportunities to Present

Project managers must interact with people on different levels in their organization, from senior executives to rank-and-file. They must present to people with expertise in different subject areas, particularly on multidisciplinary, technical projects.

They often deal with different environments. For example, the environment of a customer may be quite different from the people who build the product. They must have the ability to give effective presentations before people with different backgrounds.

Project managers must conduct different categories of meetings, some regularly scheduled and others ad hoc, to resolve issues or communicate information. They must give presentations at those meetings.

They must present during different phases of a projects life cycle. Depending on the phase, the focus of their presentations can change and frequently requires a different proposal.

Finally, project managers must give presentations at many different meetings. They must present at status review meetings, discussing and displaying the results of status collection. They must do the same at checkpoint reviews, such as achieving a major milestone to discuss performance and whether to proceed into the next phase. Likewise, they may have to present at walkthroughs, especially when reviewing and critiquing planning and scheduling details to team members and other peers. They may also have to present during "deep dives" with senior management on the details about a project. Finally, they may have to present at quality reviews to discuss the relationship of the schedule with various technical considerations.

The bottom line is that project managers present constantly and do so before different audiences of varying interests.

Loss of Effectiveness

Unfortunately, too often project managers fail at giving effective presentations, thereby losing the opportunity to maximize their effectiveness. Some ways that they dilute or eradicate their effectiveness include:

- Being too long
- Engaging in meaningless argumentative sessions
- Having no purpose or objectives for the presentation
- Having the wrong or missing attendees
- Lacking an agenda
- Letting "strong" personalities take over
- Little or no advance notification to attendees
- Not defining objectives beforehand
- Not providing a copy of the presentation
- Using jargon

One of the biggest indicators of a loss of effectiveness is the tendency of too many project managers to think that the more complex the content of a slide the greater the likelihood of clarity of thought. Nothing could be further from the truth.

Complexity indicates more confusion in thought and a lack of vision. Yet, too many times some project managers riddle their slides with so many symbols, lines, and technical terms that even experts in the room leave more confused than before, resulting in a loss of effectiveness.

Types of Presentations

Project managers essentially give three basic categories of presentations: informative, persuasive, and explanatory.

Informative presentations have the goal of communicating information (Figure 8.1). The status review session is an example of this type of presentation. During the session, status and its interpretation covers performance in respect to cost, schedule, and performance.

Persuasive presentations have the goal of convincing the audience of your way of thinking or opinion (Figure 8.2). An example is persuading senior management on the need for additional resources.

Explanatory presentations have the goal of providing an understanding about how something works (Figure 8.3). Two examples are how to enter status in a Web-based reporting tool and acquire an understanding of earned value concepts.

Characteristics of an Effective Presentation

Regardless of the type of presentation, project managers must exhibit certain characteristics of an effective presenter. Although the following list may appear incomplete, these characteristics are typical:

- Clear
- Confident
- Dynamic
- Enthusiastic
- Expressive
- Knowledgeable
- Natural
- Organized
- Pleasant
- Poised
- Positive
- Precise
- Sensitive
- Understanding

```
        I.      Title Page
        II.     Agenda
        III.    Purpose
        IV.     Status
                a.  Cumulative
                        i.  Cost
                                1.  Variances to Baseline
                                2.  Assessment
                                3.  Causes of Variances, if applicable
                        ii.  Schedule
                                1.  Variances to Baseline
                                2.  Assessment
                                3.  Causes of Variances, if applicable
                        iii.
                                1.  Variances to Baseline
                                2.  Assessment
                                3.  Causes of Variances, if applicable
                b.  Current
                        i.  Cost
                                1.  Variances to Baseline
                                2.  Assessment
                                3.  Causes of Variances, if applicable
                        ii.  Schedule
                                1.  Variances to Baseline
                                2.  Assessment
                                3.  Causes of Variances, if applicable
                        iii.  Quality Metrics
                                1.  Targets
                                2.  Variances to Targets
                                3.  Assessment
                                4.  Causes of Variances, if applicable
        V.      Recommendations for Improvement
                a.  Current
                        i.  Cost
                        ii.  Schedule
                        iii.  Quality
                b.  Cumulative
                        i.  Cost
                        ii.  Schedule
                        iii.  Quality
        VI.     Critical Issues/Action Items
        VII.    Help Needed
        VIII.   Next Steps
```

Figure 8.1   Outline of an informative presentation.

Project managers who exude confidence in themselves and the content of their presentations will be far more effective than someone who pops up with an unorganized set of slides filled with technical gibberish (Figure 8.4). When such circumstances arise and they do so, the result is poor communications. The project manager and the other stakeholders begin to argue over position rather than interests and the dialog breaks down.

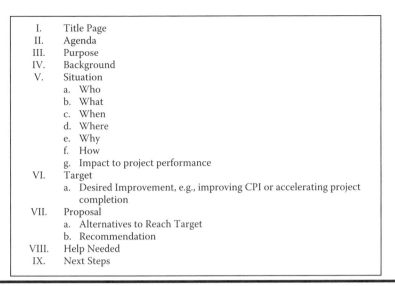

Figure 8.2   Outline of a persuasive presentation.

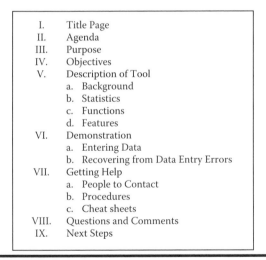

Figure 8.3   Outline of an explanatory presentation.

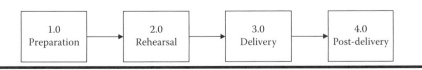

Figure 8.4   Presentation flowchart.

Preparation

Preparation is key. Without it, project managers will likely appear unorganized, unfocused, and undisciplined as well as make fulfilling their role more difficult, both as a communicator and leader (Figure 8.5).

So what is involved in preparation? Plenty:

- Determine the major participants.
- Gather background information about the presentation.
- Determine the approach towards the presentation.
- Determine the content and structure of the presentation.
- Determine visual aids.
- Prepare the presentation.

Determine the major participants. Two major participants are involved in preparation: the project manager and the audience. Both are intimately involved in the communication process.

A project must perform a self-analysis before project managers can expect to communicate effectively with the audience. This analysis requires asking questions like:

- What am I hoping to achieve from the presentation?
- What is the depth of my knowledge and understanding of the topic?
- What is my relationship with the members of the audience?
- What are my strengths vis-à-vis the audience regarding the topic?
- What are my weaknesses vis-à-vis the audience regarding the topic?

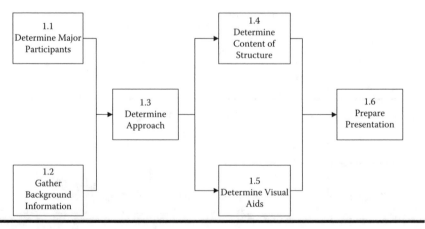

Figure 8.5   Preparation flowchart.

Project managers must also perform an analysis of the members of an audience. This analysis includes:

- Ascertaining overall knowledge, expertise, and interest level on the topic.
- Determining needs, desires, and thinking about the topic.
- Determining who might agree with the presenter, why, and develop ways to reinforce or articulate those agreements.
- Determining who might disagree with the presenter, why, and develop ideas to lessen or challenge the source of their disagreements.
- Identifying commonalities and differences among the members.
- Identifying key people.

Gather background information about the project. After determining the purpose of the presentation, project managers can ask the following fundamental questions that will help them to determine the answers about themselves and the audience.

- How long will the presentation last?
- What specifically will be the topic?
- When will the presentation occur?
- Where will the presentation occur?
- Who will attend and how many?
- Who will speak and in what order?
- Why is the presentation being delivered in the first place?

Determine the approach towards the presentation. Using the answers to the questions project managers must then develop a strategy and determine the tactics for its execution.

Strategy is determining the overall goal and structure of the presentation by focusing on two specific objectives:

- What the audience wants
- What the project wants to accomplish

Strategy is important for four reasons. It:

- Compacts a presentation
- Encourages better comprehension of its contents
- Gives cohesion to a presentation
- Leads to a better impact on the audience

Tactics are the individual actions or main points that a project manager communicates to fulfill his or her strategy.

Tactics offer three advantages. They:

- "Bridge" different ideas
- Add credibility to the presenter
- Strengthen main ideas

Determine content and structure of presentation. Once project managers know as much as possible about their presentations and their overall strategy and supporting tactics, they can start to determine the content and structure.

A key understanding of effective presentations is distinguishing and applying three essential ingredients of any presentation: pathos, ethos, and logos.

Pathos is the emotional content of a presentation (e.g., motivating members of the audience to action). *Ethos* is the "moral" or ethical content of a presentation (e.g., being truthful). *Logos* is the logical content of a presentation (e.g., organizational structure). A project management example of pathos might include persuading stakeholders to provide more resources (e.g., people to support the existing statement of work in order to impress the user community of the company's commitment to the project). An example of ethos is encouraging accurate reporting of performance even if the consequences are severe because doing so is the "right thing" to do. An example of logos is using a chain of logic (e.g., cause and effect) to do some special tasks on a project.

All presentations have all three in varying degrees of proportionality. Proportionality depends largely on the type of presentation. For example, a status review meeting will likely stress more logos and ethos than pathos. However, if the status review session also has the goal of motivating people to recover cost or schedule performance, then pathos can play an equally important role.

For most presentations in a project environment, logos has the greatest weight with ethos and pathos following in that order.

Logos (Latin for "logic") requires concentrating on the logical format to a presentation. Formats often take one of these:

- Cause and effect
- Known to unknown
- Part to whole
- Problem and solution
- Question and answer
- Simple to complex
- Time and sequence
- Topical

Using one of the logical structures described above, project managers can determine the sources of information for each main idea in a presentation.

Sources used to increase their knowledge and understanding of a subject as well as extract supporting material for a main idea in a presentation include:

- Forms
- Interviews
- Literature
- Memos

- Previous studies
- Reports
- Work papers

Often supporting data and information from the sources include statistics, examples, pictures, and diagrams. Whatever is extracted from sources, however, it must have three essential qualities:

- Brevity
- Relevancy
- Understandability

A word about statistics. Nothing can be more powerful in supporting a point than statistics. Nothing, too, can be more dangerous than a statistic because it can lose the attention of the audience. Keep these guidelines in mind when using statistics:

- Give preference to illustrations over raw numbers.
- Keep statistics to a minimum.
- Use "rounded" numbers, if possible.

Armed with sources of information, project managers are ready to build their presentation. The first important action is to understand its structure.

A presentation has three parts to it with the corresponding proportionality:

- Introduction, 10%
- Main body, 80%
- Conclusion, 10%

Introduction. This section describes the purpose, or thesis, of the presentation. It also includes the scope. In some cases, depending on the type of presentation, you can employ an attention getter. Project managers must, however, use considerable discretion in a business environment. Attention getters include:

- Demonstration
- Question
- Quotation
- Startling statement
- Story

If they desire an attention getter, such as during a kickoff meeting, project managers need to ensure it adheres to these qualities:

- Avoids giving the appearance of being immature

- Does not offend
- Has the ability to achieve the desired effect
- Is in "sync" with his or her delivery style
- Relates to the main idea of the presentation

In a project environment, the best attention getter is to state the purpose clearly and communicate the scope concisely, followed by a simple answer to the fundamental question: Why is this presentation important? Many project managers simply hold a meeting to address an issue without any clear purpose in mind. Instead, for instance, they might hold a meeting to discuss schedule problems without anyone knowing, including the project manager, what is to be accomplished exactly at the session.

The main body. This section of the presentation is the meat of a presentation. It allows project managers to support opening remarks with what is commonly referred to as "facts and data." In this section, they present the main ideas or points, each supported by relevant facts and data.

Like the overall structure of a presentation, this section should flow logically, from idea to idea. To maintain interest and further understanding it is important that the transition from one idea to another moves smoothly. A project manager can do this in several ways.

Enumeration is an effective approach. Project managers list their main ideas sequentially and then begin to talk about each one.

Subsummaries are effective. Project managers give a summary of each group of ideas up front and then progress into corresponding greater detail. This an effective approach for giving the audience an understanding of the overall gist of an idea and then "drilling down" into the details.

Starting off each point with a question is a good way to generate interest in an idea, especially if leading to a conclusion. A question raises the issue and then allows the project manager the opportunity to discuss the main idea or point in further detail.

Connective words, such as "nevertheless" and "in addition," are often used as transitions. The challenge is to use them in a way that allows each idea or point to progress meaningfully, logically. Too often, these phrases are used tritely, losing the audience rather than grabbing and maintaining their attention.

Numerous ways exists for project managers to buttress their ideas or points in the main section of a presentation. These include:

- Analogy
- Anecdotes
- Demonstrations
- Diagrams
- Examples
- Exhibits
- Expert opinion

- Facts
- Other visual aids
- Personal experience
- Statistics
- Testimonials

The significant concern is that whatever project managers use to support their ideas the material should be relevant, make it easy to see the connection, and garner support for the main idea. Failure to meet these requirements may actually weaken rather than support an idea or point.

Conclusion. A major mistake by some project managers is overlooking the importance of the conclusion. From a project management perspective, the conclusion may be the most important section of a presentation because it often leads to a fundamental question: Now what? In other words, it can serve as an effective means to encourage people to act based upon the material presented in the introduction and main body.

The contents of a conclusion may provide a summary of main ideas, a call to action, or provide a story, quote, illustration, or statistics. If using a story, quote, illustration, or statistics, project managers should make sure not just to entertain but also to support the main points of the presentation. This linkage enables the audience to see the logical flow throughout a presentation.

Project managers might consider some additional points when preparing their entire presentation, whether for the instruction, main body, or conclusion. Failure to heed its significance can lose, confuse, and even irritate some or all members of the audience:

- Avoid "fifty-cent words."
- Avoid lengthy, wordy sentences or phrases.
- Avoid trite phrases.
- Emphasize the positive but don't ignore the negative.
- Give preference to active rather than passive voice.
- Keep statistics to a minimum.
- Use adjectives and adverbs sparingly.
- Use short quotes.

Determine visual aids. Visual aids can be a project manager's best friend or worst nightmare. They are invaluable for any presentation but they are often employed clumsily.

Many types of visual aids exist. Here are some of the more common ones:

- CD and DVD
- Laptops and personal computers
- Models and mockups

- Objects
- Overhead projector and view foils
- Slide projector and slides
- Video cassettes
- White boards, chalk boards, flip charts, and wall charts

Regardless of the type of visual aid, they should all have some or all of these characteristics:

- Clean
- Clear
- Easy to use
- Manageable
- Relevant
- Understandable

The ultimate cardinal rule for visual aids, however, is that they should aid the project managers in giving a presentation and not become a liability. Unfortunately, few project managers prepare themselves on using a visual aid before giving a presentation. As a result, time is spent fumbling with the controls getting the aid ready for use during a presentation. The best advice is to determine in advance what the visual aid is, its purpose, and how to integrate its use in the presentation before using it. This common sense, of course, is frequently ignored.

Prepare the presentation. With a good solid understanding of the structure and the contents of a presentation, the next major activity is to create the presentation itself. In other words, the key determinant is to determine the means of delivery and then from there prepare the presentation.

The means of delivery depends on the degree of formality. Formal presentations require considerable more preparation than informal ones, but don't be fooled. Failure to prepare in any regard can lead to disastrous consequences for project managers.

Project managers have three fundamental means of delivery: note cards, narrative text, and outline.

Most project managers will likely never have to give a presentation using note cards or narrative text. Most of the time the presentation material will be delivered in the form of outline, or agenda, and then prepared in a slide format using a popular software tool.

Nevertheless, if note cards are necessary, use these guidelines:

- Avoid eventually playing with the cards when giving a pitch.
- Don't make their use obvious.
- Use large enough lettering.
- Use one note card per idea.
- Use the fewest number of cards possible.

If narrative text is necessary, use these guidelines:

- Avoid, if possible.
- Don't make its use obvious, by reading word for word.
- Less is better than more text, to avoid reading.

Outlining is the third means of delivery and that, too, has some guidelines to follow:

- Don't make the use of an outline obvious.
- Give it a logical flow.
- Use large enough lettering.

Whether using note cards, narrative text, or outlines here are some additional guidelines:

- Double or triple space the lines.
- Highlight or underline key words and phrases.
- Use "signposts" in the column.
- Use large type.

The key is to avoid losing one's place when giving a presentation.

Rehearsal

After preparing the presentation it would help project managers to conduct one or more rehearsals.

Several benefits are attributed to having a rehearsal, to include:

- Being natural, not contrived
- Building self-confidence and overcoming stage fright
- Controlling nervous energy
- Eliminating distracting mannerisms
- Getting comfortable with the content
- Identifying revisions to material and delivery
- Improving timing
- Learning the material
- Smoothing "rough edges"
- Synchronizing their gestures with the content
- Using visual aids

The ultimate goal, of course, is to look, feel, and sound good.

Quite often, project managers do not have the opportunity to rehearse, at least physically. However, they can do so mentally through visioning. Visioning involves finding a quiet place to sit and imagine how a presentation should go, think about what could go wrong, and formulate ways to preclude problems or how to deal with them.

If project managers have the opportunity to rehearse physically, here are a few guidelines.

Survey the site of the presentation. Look at the layout of the room, the lighting, available equipment, and the temperature. Ask: Is the layout conducive to giving the presentation effectively? If not, are improvements possible?

Recall information about the audience. If a project manager did his or her homework, the details about the audience should come easily. This information can help to determine the style or approach to adopt when giving the presentation.

Prepare the rehearsal site to reflect the actual site as much as possible. This action will generate familiarity with the surroundings and thereby increase self-confidence. However, the best option is to practice at the actual site.

Practice using visual aids and equipment. Fumbling with visual aids and equipment can prove very distracting to the audience and interfere—psychologically and physically—with getting the main points across to listeners.

Rehearse as much as possible. However, do so only to a point. A point of diminishing returns can occur if project managers do so too much; then it is likely that they will come across too perfect, even unnatural.

Visualize the presentation. At the very least, mumble the words to acquire familiarity with their flow and that of the entire presentation. The other benefit is to ensure the use of "appropriate" use of terms and phrases from the perspective of semantics and content.

Ensure the content of the presentation is clear, concise, and supportive of the message. Everything in a presentation must clearly communicate the main point. If not, remove it.

Concentrate on appearance as much as content. How project managers come across is as important as what they say. Failure to appreciate this reality will cause people to ignore the message. Body language, for example, plays a major role in the receptivity of a message.

So what should project managers look for if they get the opportunity to rehearse? Here are a few factors:

- Distracting mannerisms (e.g., hands in pockets while jingling change)
- Exceeding the time limit (e.g., providing so much data or information that it's impossible to get their point across)
- Having a illogical flow (e.g., not transitioning smoothly from one major point to another)
- Poor use of voice (e.g., coming across monotone)

- Rough or awkward delivery (e.g., not making good eye contact with the audience)
- Weak content (e.g., having content that fails to buttress sufficiently the main points)

Try to feel at ease. Take a deep breath and let the presentation flow as naturally as possible. Eliminating prejudgments will enable the "flaws" to surface, and then a project manager can address them, one by one.

Visualize how the presentation will go. This ideal image will be in project managers' subconscious and will surface naturally as they rehearse.

Concentrate on one part of a presentation at a time. Go through the entire presentation first but then work on addressing problems in each section. This will allow project managers to focus on dealing with flaws in manageable proportions.

Anticipate questions. After going through the material, try to identify questions that may arise. By anticipating the questions, project managers will be prepared to address them or weave the answers into the presentation.

Be tough. Be critical to avoid letting the ego take over. However, avoid being too critical to save one's self-confidence. The key is to strive for objectivity although it is difficult to achieve through self-evaluation.

If self-evaluation is difficult, practice with a trusted source. This person can provide the necessary feedback without devastating self-confidence. When listening to feedback, be sure to avoid making it personal. Also, recognize that a difference exists between arguing and inquiring about the reason for the feedback. If the person finds a project manager is doing the former then valuable dialogue will cease. Keep an open mind when receiving feedback and ask questions to determine the need for improvement and how to improve.

Focus on communicating ideas, not words. That requires concentrating on getting the main point across rather than the words. After mastering how to get the main points across, project managers can then work to wordsmith the presentation.

Tape the session. Give preference to video over audio. However, remember that taping, regardless of mode is quite different than a live appearance. Avoid being overly critical. A difference exists between how one comes across on tape and how one appears before a live audience. In fact, a person can look great on tape but come across contrived or "stale" before a live audience.

Practice at least three times. For some reason, three rehearsals work quite well. The first rehearsal lets the major problems surface; the second lets the project manager attempt to address problems; and the third one enables smoothing delivery.

Be positive when rehearsing. Acknowledge what is going well, too. A tendency exists to be overly critical of oneself. The reality is that project managers will likely do some aspects well, too. It is okay to recognize what they do well and they should seek ways to maximize the effect of what is done well. It also builds self-confidence.

Delivery

Delivering an effective presentation is the moment of truth. In theory, if project managers prepared and practiced sufficiently, then their delivery should be easy. Theory often doesn't match reality. However, if they fail to prepare and practice then the results can prove quite disappointing.

So assuming that project managers have prepared and practiced, what could possibly impede their effectiveness as presenters? Plenty.

Distracting mannerisms. Such mannerisms are innumerable but the more frequent ones include:

- Bracing oneself on the podium, giving the appearance of being the Leaning Tower of Pisa
- Continually combing one's fingers in the hair, as if searching for something
- Grasping pens and markers like explosives
- Holding hands in one's pockets (or worse moving them around in the pockets)
- Juggling coins in pockets
- Pacing back and forth like a walkie-talkie
- Punctuating remarks with "ahs" and "uhs"
- Snorting, coughing, and making other weird noises
- Waving pointers like an orchestra leader

Semantics. Another area that can easily impede communications when delivering a presentation is semantics, or the choice and application of words with associative meanings. How words are said and the context they're used can generate thick, tall walls between project managers and their audience. Examples include using religious, ethnic, and sexist words; vulgarity; not using everyday understandable language; and, perhaps worse, using slang. The reason why semantics is important is that it is often laden with conscious and unconscious messages, involving emotional interpretation. It can also build labels that split or polarize members of an audience, resulting in building a wall between the project manager and the audience.

Failure to apply good listening skills. In fact, this failure might be the most important because it is rarely applied even though many people talk about its importance. Examples of poor listening skills include changing a topic rather abruptly; not making effective eye contact with the appropriate people in the audience when they speak; interrupting someone before they can get their question or point across; and doing other activities while the other person is speaking.

Not considering culture. Essentially, culture reflects the values, beliefs, and behaviors of a group of people. Culture can affect the quality of the message being sent or received between yourself and the audience. Three common areas to consider are race, ethnicity, and religion. There are, however, more "softer" cultural considerations, to include management style, perceptions about issues, mores, and morals.

Unsatisfactory physical environment. The physical environment can impede effective communications. Factors indicative of an unsatisfactory physical environment include poor lighting, people crammed in a small area, the ambient temperature being too cold or hot, too much background noise, and the surroundings being too messy.

Declining memory of the audience. This factor can impede presentations. How? The fact is that, although the mind is a fantastic information processor, its memory can be quite short. The longer the presentation the more difficult an audience has in retaining what was said. Fortunately, here are some guidelines for increasing the memory of an audience:

- Coordinate gestures with a word or phrase.
- Emphasize a word or phrase by either italicizing or bolding it on a slide or altering the sound of one's voice when uttering it.
- Emphasize key points through body movement and voice.
- Employ metaphors, analogies, and associations.
- Employ repetition.
- Encourage audience participation.
- Have a strong opening or ending that references the context within the body of the presentation.

Setting the stage is very important to get a project off to smooth start. Project managers can achieve that in four ways:

- Identify the best times to give a presentation.
- Determine the appropriate room configuration.
- Provide seating for the desired effect.
- Try to arrive early.

Identify the best times to give a presentation. If lucky, project managers will have the option to determine the best time to give their presentation. If not, then they must be able to acknowledge to themselves why the time is not the best and adjust the content of their presentation accordingly. Ideally, the most effective times to give a presentation is during the mornings of Tuesday, Wednesday, and Thursday. The periods to avoid are Mondays, Fridays, anytime just before or after lunch, and close to the end of a working day. If project managers have no other choice, then they can make adjustments in their delivery or content or try to reschedule to a more appropriate time.

Try to arrive early. It is highly encouraged to arrive early at the presentation site. This will give project managers ample time to not only set up equipment but to make the electronic connections (e.g., laptop connection to the Internet). Project managers will also have the opportunity to check out other considerations, including:

- Equipment
- Lighting
- Potential disruptive noises (e.g., sound of HVAC equipment)
- Room arrangement
- Sound system
- Surroundings (e.g., temperature)

If given the chance, project managers should check the scene even before rehearsal. That way, they will get a feel for the ambience or atmosphere. With that knowledge, they can rehearse in a manner that reflects the environment where the presentation will occur.

Determine the appropriate room configuration. Configuration of the room can affect the degree of receptivity of the members of the audience towards the message. Project managers should consider looking for these items when arriving early to give the presentation:

- Equipment
- Layout
- Lighting
- Quietude
- Seating
- Size
- Spacing
- Supplies
- Temperature

Provide seating for the type of presentation. Several types of configurations of the seating of a room can exist. The following heuristics are useful to determine the best seating arrangement:

- If a workshop atmosphere is desirable, sit five or six people at a round table
- Less than 25 people, U-shaped
- More than 25, classroom
- To encourage everyone to sit together, remove all empty chairs

During the delivery, project managers should pay attention to presenting the "right" image to the audience. Two important factors to consider for presenting this image are:

- Placing importance on credibility
- Presenting a positive image

Place importance on credibility. Project managers often discount the importance of converging or reenforcing credibility. They assume that people will automatically grant it to them. Yet, nothing is more precious to preserve or reenforce in project management. Tarnish or lose one's credibility and the message gets lost, along with any request for action.

During a presentation, project managers have many opportunities to lose credibility. Often, much of the loss of credibility has much to do with content. For example, credibility can decline or disappear if the content:

- Contains incomplete information
- Includes conflicting data vis-à-vis the message being communicated
- Is disorganized (e.g., no logical sequence)
- Is inaccurate
- Possesses irrelevant data
- Uses unclear examples and diagrams (e.g., too much clutter on a slide)

Present a positive image. Not only can content destroy one's credibility, but so can one's very own qualities. This factor is often overlooked because many project managers rely on the "facts and data." Although important, a negative appearance or behavior can harm any solid set of facts and data. Here are some guidelines to follow to avoid hurting or losing credibility when presenting:

- Avoid being apologetic and presenting "sob stories."
- Back your voice with confident, supporting body language.
- Be clear and concise.
- Be positive.
- Have a clean, well-groomed appearance (e.g., dress neatly).
- Maintain eye contact with the members of the audience.
- Speak in a strong, clear voice.

Project managers, like so many other presenters, want to avoid stage fright. Although it can wreak havoc on the nerves, stage fright can be their best friend if controlled. How can project managers control it? By directing their nervousness into their presentations.

Most people, too, have little difficulty in detecting whether they have a case of stage fright. Nevertheless, here are some of the overt symptoms:

- Being tongue-tied
- Feeling faint
- Grabbing the podium
- Having "butterflies" in the stomach
- Having a dry throat
- Having an unrealistic fear, e.g., people pointing fingers at you and laughing

- Having sweaty palms and forehead
- Making inappropriate statements
- Turning "pink"

Of course, project managers do not have to feel paralyzed by stage fright before or during the presentation. Here are some guidelines for dealing with it:

- Direct nervousness into body language.
- Direct the nervousness into the presentation.
- Get plenty of rest the previous night.
- Learn as much as possible about the audience before delivering your presentation.
- Mingle with members of the audience prior to presenting.
- Recognize it's a natural feeling.
- Take a deep breathe before the audience.
- Treat the entire audience as a complete entity unto itself and not simply a composite of individuals.
- View members of the audience as "friends" or "peers," not as evaluators.
- Visit the room before presenting to feel comfortable.

After recognizing the importance of dealing with stage fright and converting it into your "best friend," project managers are ready to deliver. Opening and closing of a presentation share many characteristics that will be discussed together. These shared characteristics include:

- Be brief.
- Be direct.
- Be relevant.
- Communicate why they should listen or take action.
- Memorize, if possible.
- Relate to the audience.
- Start or finish on time.
- Use attention getters.

Use attention getters. Project managers should use discretion here. Using attention getters does not mean being outlandish. Rather, it means saying or doing something that communicates clearly the purpose of the presentation. Avoid being "cute." If project managers insist on using attention getters, they should use examples (e.g., diagrams, illustrations, and facts and data) to highlight the topic they will discuss.

Be brief and direct. Nothing is more compelling for an opening than stating the purpose of the meeting, clearly and concisely, to include goals and objectives. Nothing grabs the attention more than describing up front the purpose and the desired result. This is especially the case when project managers must present before executives or customers.

Be relevant. If project managers must use an attention getter, ensure that it is relevant and doesn't offend anyone. Some project managers like to start or end a presentation with a joke; this tactic is dangerous for three reasons. One, the joke must be relevant to the topic (which is infrequent). Two, the joke may fall flat or offend someone. Third, it may hurt the project manager's credibility by trivializing the purpose or the need for action.

Start or finish on time. Nothing communicates unimportance or disregard towards the audience more than not starting on time and, especially, showing up late. Both actions communicate the wrong message that something or someone is more important than the audience.

Exceeding the allotted time is just as bad. It communicates that the project managers feel superior, and it conveys disrespect for the importance of the audience's time. The best approach is to finish earlier than the allotted time. By doing so, it enables the audience to "hunger" for additional information or allow them time to absorb the message.

Memorize, if possible. The goal is to "grab" the attention of the audience to involve them emotionally with the project managers and their message. In addition, the members of the audience will likely want to act on the message, thereby reflecting the degree of their emotional involvement.

Memorization of both the introduction and conclusion makes it easier for project managers to gain that emotional involvement. However, there is a downside to memorization. Project managers may become too smooth and, therefore, come across contrived or lackluster. The key is to know what they want to say, say it with conviction, and worry less about exact recital of content.

Communicate why they should listen or take action. The opening should clearly convey the topic. People should not have to "fish around" to discover the purpose. State the issue clearly and concisely and, if necessary, then present additional facts and data.

The closing should reiterate the purpose of the presentation but, more importantly, not leave the audience "hanging." The closing should impel them to action in some way. Don't just tell them, for instance, that there is a problem or an issue exists. Give the audience options and even select the best one. Too often, project managers come up with a problem but fail to present options and even a recommendation.

Relate to the audience. This point applies to all aspects of the presentation but even more so during the introduction and conclusion. Here are some common guidelines for relating to the audience, particularly during the introduction and conclusion:

- Avoid jargon and esoteric terms.
- Be clear and concise.
- Be conversational.

- Be logical.
- Don't be condescending or pedantic.
- Position yourself as close to the audience as possible.
- Synchronize emotional content with physical activity.
- Use concepts, illustrations, etc. that they can relate to and understand.
- Use their language, not your own.

Project managers will likely find it difficult enough to relate to the audience during the introduction and conclusion. It can be equally, if not more, challenging keeping the audience attentive to their comments. Here are some guidelines to keep the audience attentive during a presentation:

- Apply ways to wake up an audience.
- Avoid surefire ways to put an audience to sleep.
- Employ physical actions.
- Maintain effective eye contact.
- Recognize ways to turn off an audience.
- Sustain audience interest.
- Use humor.
- Use vocal variety.

Recognize ways to turn off an audience. Dealing with an audience is always wrought with danger. Rewards can be immense if everything goes right but it can quickly turn negative if problems arise. Here are some guidelines on what not to do or to avoid for turning off an audience:

- "Dumping" meaningless statistics
- Being arrogant
- Being pompous
- Being sarcastic
- Insulting
- Making excuses
- Reading text
- Ridiculing
- Telling personal problems

Avoid surefire ways to put an audience to sleep. One of the most common and obvious indicators that an audience is falling asleep is the constant nodding of heads. Yet, many project managers seem oblivious to what is happening. Of course, if one or two individuals in the audience find themselves falling asleep it may be due to other reasons beyond the control of project managers. If it happens to many members of an audience, then a problem exists.

Here are some additional indicators to look for to assess whether one is putting a good share of the audience asleep:

- Avoiding eye contact
- Hiding behind the podium
- Lacking enthusiasm
- Not involving the audience
- Not using gestures
- Reading a presentation
- Reading from visual aids
- Taking infrequent breaks
- Talking in jargon
- Using a monotone voice
- Using statistics profusely

Apply ways to wake up an audience. Of course, even the best project managers will put an audience to sleep at least once in their careers. If most of the members of an audience begin to fall asleep, here are some guidelines to enliven the presentation:

- Change a statement into a question
- Employ more body movement and vocal variety
- Encourage some physical or social interaction
- Give more frequent breaks
- Present some mental challenges
- Walk into the audience

Sustain audience interest. Even if project managers have the attention of the audience, they still have the challenge of sustaining it. Sustaining interest is perhaps the biggest challenge because people's attention span is limited and affected by many factors that a project manager may or may not have control over. Here are some guidelines for sustaining the interest of the audience:

- Add emotion with logic.
- Give frequent breaks.
- Keep eye contact with the audience.
- Refer to notes sparingly.
- Show enthusiasm and smile.
- Use "signal" words.
- Use body language.
- Use pauses.
- Use repetition.
- Use simple language.
- Vary use of voice.

Use humor. Although humor can enlighten and enliven a presentation, project managers should apply it with discretion. The tone of some presentations may not be conducive to using humor; under such circumstances, they should avoid it. If circumstances allow it, humor may be a useful tool to get people to accept and act upon what they say. Here are guidelines for using humor:

- Avoid pointless humor, that is, being unrelated to the goals and objectives of the presentation.
- Don't let humor overshadow the main goals and objectives.
- Ensure that your humor is inoffensive. (Follow the motto: when in doubt, leave it out.)
- Use positive rather than negative humor.
- Use short rather than long jokes.

Use physical action. Movement before an audience can prove quite useful during a presentation, especially if covering a boring topic being delivered during a "bad" time period (e.g., just after lunch). The right physical action can help to keep the audience awake, dramatize and emphasize meanings and main ideas, dissipate any nervous tension, and clarify messages.

Using physical action requires an acute awareness of project managers' physical presence before an audience and requires the conscious ability to adjust their activity via five physical actions: eye contact, voice, facial expressions, gestures, and body movement.

Eye contact is perhaps the most important. Sustaining eye contact makes it very difficult for the members of an audience to pay less attention to your message. Eye contact involves, however, more than merely looking at someone. Here are some guidelines to ensure effective eye contact:

- Acknowledge feedback, especially by observing the body language of members in the audience.
- Avoid reading a presentation off a screen or notes.
- Know your material so eye contact is easier.
- Look at someone per idea.
- Look into the audience without focusing on just one person.
- Don't use "artificial" means to maintain eye contact (e.g., fixation on an object in the corners of the room).

If, for some reason, project managers must read parts of their presentations, here are some steps to follow:

1. Look down or up at the material but say nothing to generate interest in what is about to be said.
2. Remember just a portion of a phrase.

3. Look up at the audience.
4. Pause briefly.
5. Say the phrase and then read the remainder of the sentence.

Use one's voice. Next to eye contact, the voice becomes the project managers' most powerful presentation tool. They can use it to emphasize or de-emphasize material or encourage a desired reaction by people (e.g., excitement or relaxation). Here are some guidelines for using their voice effectively:

- For articulation, do so clearly.
- For pace, be moderate (e.g., 125 to 160 words per minute).
- For pitch, be normal.
- For volume, be conversational.

Of course, project managers want to avoid the worse when using their voice: speaking in a monotone and being hard to understand. Therefore, they should make every effort to employ vocal variety but naturally and, above all, apply their voice in a manner synchronized with their message (e.g., talking in an excited way when communicating an insignificant issue). Synchronization is very important, too, with your voice to establish and sustain credibility with the audience.

The presentations of many project managers have visual aids, usually in the form of view foils, flip charts and film and video (rarely), and overhead projectors. Project managers should conscientiously use these aids in the delivery of their presentation.

Interestingly, visual aids are often used to clarify and further the effectiveness of a presentation, but so often project managers add confusion. Here are common pitfalls to avoid that can interfere with their message:

- Having slides or view foils with a font size that is too small for members in the back room to see.
- Having view foils or slides containing irrelevant data that detracts from the information.
- Having view foils or slides packed or, more accurately, cluttered with data.
- Having view foils or slides with contents that do not contrast with the background.
- Leaning on the visual aid (e.g., projector equipment, and then having to reposition it).
- Letting equipment operate (e.g., view foil projector shooting a blank image on the screen while the presenter talks about another idea or topic).
- Not setting up equipment prior to the presentation but doing so during the opening.
- Operating equipment or moving from view foil or sliding out of the intended sequence.

- Position equipment in such a way that a few people cannot see the information projected (e.g., blocking line of sight).
- Talk to the visual aid when you should make visual contact with the audience.

These are common pitfalls that seem to plague many presentations. Although some seem insignificant, project managers must look at them from the perspective of their audience. From the listeners'/viewers' perspective, the focus moves from the message to the action. Members can become frustrated, too, and generate mental blocks about what the project managers say. Here are some common guidelines to consider when employing specific types of visual aids.

For using the overhead projector and other types of projectors:

- Avoid blocking the projected image, either by the presenter or members of the audience.
- Avoid making the room pitch black; it invites people to nap.
- Connect all outlets before giving a presentation.
- Keep an extra bulb handy.
- Keep extra writing pens handy (for overhead projectors).
- Know how to replace the bulb or specific types of equipment to avoid fumbling while giving a presentation.
- Position an image so everyone in the audience can see it.
- Turn the device off when not in use.

For using view foils and slides:

- Avoid cluttering.
- Consider masking bullets until they become the topic to discuss (however, do so judiciously because it can become tiresome and irksome).
- Employ color to emphasize a point and do so sparingly.
- Ensure the background is light and clean.
- Give preference to pictures over words.
- Keep the slide simple.
- Never quote verbatim, if possible.
- Only leave relevant images showing.
- Pause prior to and after presenting a slide.

Use handouts. Frequently, handouts are documents. To communicate effectively these documents should be clear, concise, and understandable. They also serve as an excellent means for providing minutes or an audit trail of the message. Here are some guidelines for using handouts effectively:

- Avoid reading them directly when referring to them during the presentation.

■ Distribute them at the very start or end of a presentation, preferably the latter to keep their attention on the project managers and their message.
■ Ensure that their presentation is in concert with the content, both in terms of flow and message.
■ Give individual members of the audience their own copy.

Use flip charts. This visual aid can prove the most useful; however, it can cause considerable disruption. Flip charts are useful to engage the audience and communicate the message. However, often flip chart usage fails because project managers fail to prepare in advance on their usage, e.g., not putting up the stand before the presentation, or having an insufficient number of flip chart pads of paper available. To use flip charts effectively, follow these guidelines:

■ Ensure the print is legible so everyone can read the content.
■ Record in the pad as much as possible before the presentation and then fill in what is necessary.
■ Use different colors to augment the message.
■ Use every other page to record message to avoid bleeding on the next page and blending in with the previous page.
■ Use white paper to get the necessary contrast for seeing the writing.
■ Write key words and phrases, not long sentences.

Use film and video. More often than not, project managers will likely not have to use film and video. If they do, it will likely be about a topic like earned value or using a status update tool. If project managers find themselves having to use film or video, such as DVDs or CDs, follow these guidelines:

■ Consider using more than one monitor per 25 people so everyone can watch.
■ Explain the purpose of the film or video.
■ Summarize the main points afterwards.

Post Delivery

One of the most challenging and nervous circumstances when giving a presentation is answering questions. How well project managers answer questions will affect their persuasiveness with listeners. In fact, project managers can give the "best" presentation ever but if they fail to answer any question or feign one, they will lose credibility.

Questions, of course, are good despite the anxiety they cause. They help project managers to clarify points; build and sustain a relationship with the audience; communicate additional data and information; and reiterate important points.

Here are some guidelines to follow when answering questions:

- Announce beforehand whether people can ask questions during or after the presentation.
- Rephrase or repeat a question, if necessary, to clarify one's understanding and for others.
- Admit it if you do not know an answer or better yet, say you will follow up (and do so).
- Pause before responding to think about a response (not as easy as you think) and to convey to the questioner the importance of the question.
- Do not leave immediately after the presentation, because some are shy about asking questions within a group but might feel more comfortable after the audience breaks up.
- Allow members of an audience to answer a question to ascertain whether a message was understood and that they are emotionally involved.
- Provide short and simple answers rather than long and complex.

Summary

Project managers communicate 90 percent of their time, frequently before an audience. To give effective presentations, they must follow three simple actions that require a considerable work.

First, they must prepare. They must know their audience as much as possible and develop and organize their material in a manner that augments, rather than strays, from their main message. Too often, project managers think all they have to do is put a few slides on a projector screen and the rest will fall in place. This thinking is reflected in the often poor presentations given at project meetings.

Second, they must rehearse. Project managers must envision the presentation and then practice, practice, and practice. Avoid the temptation of taking the easy way out and not practicing presentation skills as much as some project managers do with planning and scheduling. A sloppy delivery can result in poor acceptance of facts and data, no matter how convincing you think your logic is. To rehearse effectively, you should replicate in the rehearsal environment that of the actual presentation; do several rehearsals, if necessary, and concentrate on synchronizing voice, body, movement, and content.

Third, project managers must deliver their message with as much determination and focus as achieving the goals and objectives of a project. Their delivery should strive to acquire and maintain interest, control nervousness, be as natural as possible, be positive rather than negative, and, above all, view the presentation as an opportunity rather than a threat.

Getting Started Checklist		
Question	*Yes*	*No*
1. Have you managed to avoid these ways to dilute the effectiveness of presentations:		
Being too long?		
Engaging in meaningless argumentative sessions?		
Having no purpose or objectives for the presentation?		
Having the wrong or missing attendees?		
Lacking an agenda?		
Letting "strong" personalities take over?		
Little or no advance notification to attendees?		
2. Do you give any of these types of presentations?		
Explanatory?		
Informative?		
Persuasive?		
3. Do your presentations have any of these characteristics (or need to improve upon)?		
Clear?		
Confident?		
Dynamic?		
Enthusiastic?		
Expressive?		
Knowledgeable?		
Natural?		
Organized?		
Pleasant?		
Poised?		
Positive?		
Precise?		
Sensitive?		
Understanding?		
4. When preparing for presentations, do you perform these activities?		
Determine the major participants?		
Gather background information?		
Determine the approach?		

Getting Started Checklist (Continued)		
Question	*Yes*	*No*
Determine content and structure?		
Determine visual aids?		
Prepare the presentation in one of these formats:		
Cards?		
Narrative text?		
Outline?		
5. When determining major participants, do you do the following?		
Perform a self analysis by answering questions like:		
What am I hoping to achieve from the presentation?		
What is my relationship with the members of the audience?		
What is my strengths vis-à-vis the audience regarding the topic?		
What are my weaknesses vis-à-vis the audience regarding the topic?		
What is the depth of my knowledge and understanding of the topic?		
Answer questions about the audience concerning:		
Their overall knowledge, expertise, and interest level on the topic		
Needs, desires, and thinking about the topic		
Who might agree with the presenter, why, and develop ways to reenforce or articulate those agreements		
Who might disagree with the presenter, why, and develop ideas to lessen or challenge the source of their disagreements		
Commonalities and differences among the members		
Key people		
6. When gathering background information, do you consider the following?		
How long will the presentation last?		
What specifically will be the topic?		
When will the presentation occur?		
Where will the presentation occur?		
Who will attend and how many?		
Who will speak and in what order?		

Getting Started Checklist (Continued)			
Question		Yes	No
	Why is the presentation being delivered in the first place?		
7.	When determining the approach, do you consider the following?		
	Strategy		
	Tactics		
8.	When determining content and structure, do you consider these?		
	Logos		
	Pathos		
	Structure		
9.	For logos, do you consider the following?		
	Cause and effect		
	Known to unknown		
	Part to whole		
	Problem and solution		
	Question and answer		
	Simple to complex		
	Time and sequence		
	Topical		
10.	Do you consider the following items for background information to support logos?		
	Forms		
	Interviews		
	Literature		
	Memos		
	Previous studies		
	Reports		
	Work papers		
11.	When developing the introduction, do you consider these?		
	Attention getters like a:		
	Demonstration		
	Question		
	Quotation		
	Startling statement		
	When using an attention getter, does it have these qualities?		

Getting Started Checklist (Continued)			
Question		*Yes*	*No*
	Avoids giving the appearance of being immature		
	Does not offend		
	Has the ability to achieve the desired effect		
	Is in "sync" with your delivery style		
	Relates to the main idea of the presentation		
12.	When developing the main body, do you support major ideas or points with these?		
	Analogy		
	Anecdotes		
	Demonstrations		
	Diagrams		
	Examples		
	Exhibits		
	Expert opinion		
	Facts		
	Personal experience		
	Statistics		
	Testimonials		
13.	If using cards for your presentation, do you consider the following?		
	Avoid eventually playing with the cards when giving a pitch?		
	Don't make their use obvious?		
	Use large enough lettering?		
	Use one note card per idea?		
	Use the fewest number of cards possible?		
14.	If using narrative text, do you consider:		
	Avoid making its use obvious?		
	Think less is better than more text?		
15.	If using an outline, are you—		
	Not making its use obvious?		
	Giving it a logical flow?		
	Using large enough lettering?		
16.	Whether using cards, narrative text, or outlines, do you consider:		
	Double or triple spacing the lines?		

Getting Started Checklist (Continued)			
Question		Yes	No
	Highlighting or underlining key words and phrases?		
	Using "signposts" in the column?		
	Using large type?		
17.	When rehearsing, do you follow these guidelines?		
	Survey the site of the presentation?		
	Recall information about the audience?		
	Prepare the rehearsal site to reflect the actual as much as possible?		
	Practice using visual aids and equipment?		
	Rehearse as much as possible?		
	Visualize the presentation?		
	Ensure that the content is clear, concise, and supportive of the message?		
	Concentrate on appearance as much as content?		
	Try to feel at ease?		
	Concentrate on one part of the presentation at a time?		
	Anticipate questions?		
	Be tough?		
	Focus on communicating ideas, not words?		
	Tape the session?		
	Practice at least three times?		
	Be positive?		
18.	When delivering a presentation, do you consider impediments to effectiveness, like:		
	Appropriate room configuration?		
	Best times to give a presentation?		
	Declining memory of the audience?		
	Distracting mannerisms?		
	Failure to apply good listening skills?		
	Ignoring culture?		
	Semantics?		
	Setting the stage?		
	Trying to arrive early?		
	Unsatisfactory physical environment?		

Getting Started Checklist (Continued)		
Question	Yes	No
19. When presenting, do you find yourself having these distracting mannerisms:		
Bracing oneself on the podium, giving the appearance of being the Leaning Tower of Pisa?		
Continually combing one's fingers in the hair, as if searching for something?		
Grasping pens and markers as if they were explosives?		
Holding hands in one's pockets (or worse, moving them around in the pockets)?		
Juggling coins in pockets?		
Pacing back and forth like a walkie-talkie?		
Punctuating remarks with "ahs" and "uhs"?		
Snorting, coughing, and making other weird noises?		
Waving pointers like an orchestra leader?		
20. If concerned about the declining memory of the audience, do you:		
Coordinate gestures with a word or phrase?		
Emphasize a word or phrase by either italicizing or bolding it on a slide or altering the sound of one's voice when uttering it?		
Emphasize key points through body movement and voice?		
Employ metaphors, analogies, and associations?		
Employ repetition?		
Encourage audience participation?		
Have a strong opening or ending that references the context within the body of the presentation?		
21. If you look at the presentation site beforehand, do you:		
Place importance on credibility?		
Present a positive image?		
22. Do you consider ways that you could hurt your credibility like:		
Containing incomplete information?		
Including conflicting data vis-à-vis the message being communicated?		
Being disorganized (e.g., no logical sequence)?		
Being inaccurate?		
Possessing irrelevant data?		

Getting Started Checklist (Continued)			
Question		Yes	No
	Using unclear examples and diagrams (e.g., too much clutter on a slide)?		
	Containing incomplete information?		
	Including conflicting data vis-à-vis the message being communicated?		
23.	When looking at room configuration, do you consider:		
	Equipment?		
	Layout?		
	Lighting?		
	Quietude?		
	Seating?		
	Size?		
	Spacing?		
	Supplies?		
	Temperature?		
24.	When looking at seating, do you consider:		
	Less than 25 people?		
	More than 25?		
	Encouraging everyone to sit together?		
25.	When giving a presentation, do you exhibit stage fright like:		
	Being tongue-tied?		
	Feeling faint?		
	Grabbing the podium?		
	Having "butterflies" in the stomach?		
	Having a dry throat?		
	Having an unrealistic fear (e.g., people pointing fingers at you and laughing)?		
	Having sweaty palms and forehead?		
	Making inappropriate statements?		
	Turning "pink"?		
26.	To overcome stage fright do you:		
	Direct nervousness into body language?		
	Direct the nervousness into the presentation?		
	Get plenty of rest the previous night?		

Getting Started Checklist (Continued)			
Question		Yes	No
	Learn as much as possible about the audience before delivering your presentation?		
	Mingle with members of the audience prior to presenting?		
	Recognize it's a natural feeling?		
	Take a deep breathe before addressing the audience?		
	Treat the entire audience as a complete entity unto itself and not simply a composite of individuals?		
	View members of the audience as "friends" or "peers," not as evaluators?		
	Visit the room before presenting to feel comfortable?		
27.	For opening and closing presentations, do you remind yourself to:		
	Be brief?		
	Be direct?		
	Be relevant?		
	Communicate why the audience should listen or take action?		
	Memorize, if possible?		
	Relate to the audience?		
	Start or finish on time?		
	Use attention getters?		
28.	Do you consider any of these ways to keep the audience attentive:		
	Apply ways to wake up an audience?		
	Avoid surefire ways to put an audience to sleep?		
	Employ physical action?		
	Maintain effective eye contact?		
	Recognize ways to turn off an audience?		
	Sustain audience interest?		
	Use humor?		
	Use vocal variety?		
29.	So as not to turn off an audience, do you avoid:		
	"Dumping" meaningless statistics?		
	Being arrogant?		
	Being pompous?		
	Being sarcastic?		

Getting Started Checklist (Continued)		Yes	No
Question			
	Insulting?		
	Making excuses?		
	Reading text?		
	Ridiculing?		
	Telling personal problems?		
30.	Do you consider these ways to relate to an audience:		
	Avoid jargon and esoteric terms?		
	Be clear and concise?		
	Be conversational?		
	Be logical?		
	Don't be condescending or pedantic?		
	Position yourself as close to the audience as possible?		
	Synchronize emotional content with physical activity?		
	Use concepts, illustrations, etc., that they can relate to and understand?		
	Use their language, not your own?		
31.	Do you perform any of the following that can put an audience to sleep:		
	Avoiding eye contact?		
	Hiding behind the podium?		
	Lacking enthusiasm?		
	Not involving the audience?		
	Not using gestures?		
	Reading a presentation?		
	Reading from visual aids?		
	Taking infrequent breaks?		
	Talking in jargon?		
	Using a monotone voice?		
	Using statistics profusely?		
32.	Do you consider these items for sustaining audience interest:		
	Add emotion with logic?		
	Give frequent breaks?		
	Keep eye contact with the audience?		
	Refer to notes sparingly?		

	Getting Started Checklist (Continued)	Yes	No
	Question	*Yes*	*No*
	Show enthusiasm and smile?		
	Use "signal" words?		
	Use body language?		
	Use pauses?		
	Use repetition?		
	Use simple language?		
	Vary use of voice?		
33.	If you want to use humor, do you:		
	Avoid pointless humor that is unrelated to the goals and objectives of the presentation?		
	Don't let humor overshadow the main goals and objectives?		
	Ensure that your humor is inoffensive? (Follow the motto "When in doubt, leave it out."?)		
	Use positive rather than negative humor?		
	Use short rather than long jokes?		
34.	To ensure effective eye contact, do you:		
	Acknowledge feedback, especially by observing the body language of members in the audience?		
	Avoid reading a presentation off a screen or notes?		
	Know your material so eye contact is easier?		
	Look at someone per thought?		
	Look into the audience without focusing on just one person?		
	Not use "artificial" means to maintain eye contact (e.g., fixation on an object in the corners of the room)?		
35.	If you must read your presentation, do you:		
	Look down or up at the material but say nothing to generate interest in what you are about to say?		
	Remember just a portion of a phrase?		
	Look up at the audience?		
	Pause briefly?		
	Say the phrase?		
	Read the remainder of the sentence?		
36.	Do you consider these elements for using your voice:		
	For articulation, do so clearly?		
	For pace, be moderate (e.g., 125 to 160 words per minute)?		

Getting Started Checklist (Continued)		
Question	*Yes*	*No*
For pitch, be normal?		
For volume, be conversational?		
37. Do you avoid these pitfalls when using slides or view foils:		
Have slides or view foils with a font size that is too small for members in the back of the room to see?		
Have view foils or slides containing irrelevant data which detracts from the information?		
Have view foils or slides with contents that do not contrast with the background?		
Lean on the visual aid (e.g., projector equipment) and then have to reposition it?		
Let equipment operate (e.g., view foil projector shooting a blank image on the screen while the presenter talks about another idea or topic)?		
Not set up equipment prior to the presentation but do so during the opening?		
Operate equipment or move the view foil or slide out of the intended sequence?		
Position equipment in such a way that a few people cannot see the information projected (e.g., blocking line of sight)?		
Talk to the visual aid when you should make visual contact with the audience?		
38. When using projector equipment, do you:		
Avoid blocking the projected image, either by the presenter or members of the audience?		
Avoid making the room pitch black (it invites people to nap)?		
Connect all outlets before giving a presentation?		
Keep an extra bulb handy?		
Keep extra writing pens handy (for overhead projectors)?		
Know how to replace the bulb or specific types of equipment to avoid fumbling while giving a presentation?		
Position an image so everyone in the audience can see it?		
Turn the device off when not in use?		
39. When using view foils and slides, do you:		
Avoid cluttering?		

	Getting Started Checklist (Continued)		
	Question	Yes	No
	Consider masking bullets until they become the topic to discuss (however, do so judiciously because it can become tiresome and irksome)?		
	Employ color to emphasize a point and do so sparingly?		
	Ensure the background is light and clean?		
	Give preference to pictures over words?		
	Keep the slide simple?		
	Never quote verbatim, if possible?		
	Only leave relevant images showing?		
	Pause prior to and after presenting a slide?		
40.	To use handouts effectively, do you:		
	Avoid reading them directly when referring to them during the presentation?		
	Distribute them at the very start or end of a presentation, preferably the latter, to keep their attention on the project manager and his or her message?		
	Ensure that your presentation is in concert with the content, both in terms of flow and message?		
	Give individual members of the audience their own copy?		
41.	When using flip charts, do you:		
	Ensure your print is legible so everyone can read what you write?		
	Record in the pad as much as possible before the presentation and then fill in what is necessary?		
	Use different colors to augment your message?		
	Use every other page to record message to avoid bleeding on the next page and blending in with the previous page?		
	Use white paper to get the necessary contrast for seeing your writing?		
	Write key words and phrases, not long sentences?		
42.	When using film or video, do you:		
	Consider using more than one monitor per 25 people so everyone can watch?		
	Explain the purpose of the film or video?		
	Summarize the main points afterwards?		

Getting Started Checklist (Continued)			
Question		*Yes*	*No*
43.	When answering questions, do you:		
	Admit it if one does not know an answer or better yet, say he or she will follow up (and do so)?		
	Allow members of an audience to answer a question to ascertain whether a message was understood and that they are emotionally involved?		
	Announce beforehand whether people can ask questions during or after the presentation?		
	Do not leave immediately after the presentation because some are shy about asking questions within a group but might feel more comfortable after the audience breaks up?		
	Pause before responding to think about a response (not as easy as you think) and to convey to the questioner the importance of the question?		
	Provide short and simple answers rather than long and complex?		
	Rephrase or repeat a question, if necessary, to clarify one's understanding and for others?		

Chapter 9

Developing and Deploying a Web Site

The Internet is one of the major revolutions of the modern world. It has dramatically changed the way people communicate, and this impact is especially exhibited when managing projects.

PMIS Contributions

A PMIS can provide material for a project Web site. This material can include cost and schedule reports, policies and procedures, organization charts, presentations, and data tables. A challenge is determining what materials can appear on a Web site as opposed to material restricted to only a few people. The other challenge is ensuring that what appears on the Web site reflects what's in the PMIS.

Three Main Advantages

A project Web site provides three principal advantages.

It can make data and information available to everyone needing it. Stakeholders can readily access, for example, schedule reports, forms to collect data, and status information. This advantage can prove very powerful for project managers. Not only does it alleviate the administrative burden on project managers but it also gives them an added benefit. They can indirectly place pressure on stakeholders who fail to perform on a project. For example, a stakeholder may refuse to status the schedule while all the others do so. The project manager can then display the results on a Web site, reflecting all stakeholders' performance relative to one another. The stakeholder not complying, for example, will likely have a lower schedule or cost performance index.

A project Web site also can also help in giving visibility to a project. Project managers can place individual and group status on the Web site. This status can engender responsibility and accountability because other people can see their own performance and the impact on others. For example, project managers can develop reports that center on the critical path based upon the predecessor relationships among tasks. By displaying the appropriate report, project managers can highlight which schedule slides impact the performance of others. The display of this information on a Web site can place considerable pressure on stakeholders to perform according to schedule.

Finally, a project Web site helps to engender a sense of team identity. It accomplishes that by allowing people to "show off their stuff" as a team. Team members can add information and deliverables to gain recognition for individuals or the entire team. Examples include procedures and standards that a team developed for a project, results of a major delivery to a customer, and even pictures of individuals who have exceeded the norm.

Two Main Challenges

Having a project Web site presents two challenges despite its advantages.

The first challenge is keeping the Web site current. A project by its very nature involves change and during its life cycle considerable change occurs, from people to performance. The content of the Web site can easily and quickly become out-dated, such as data, information, and links to other sites. To ensure the currency of the site, assign a role and responsibility for regular updating.

The other challenge is some stakeholders may lack the ability to access a site. Reasons include not having the appropriate software, hardware, or access lines; lack of knowledge on how to access a Web site; or proprietary restrictions. Project managers along with their Webmasters should explore ways to ensure that everyone has access to a site. Stakeholders lacking access will have to set up an alternative means (e.g., placing data and information on a server or sending both as attachments in e-mails).

Important Guidelines

To maximize value of a project Web site, follow these guidelines (Figure 9.1).

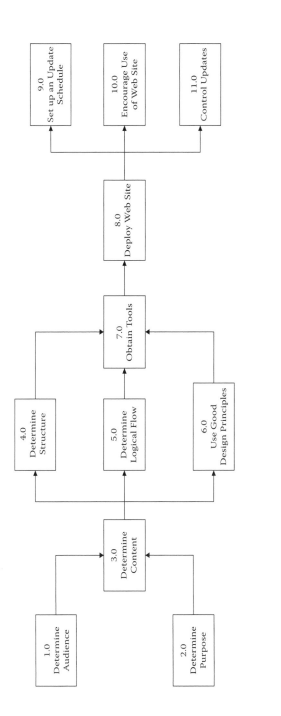

Figure 9.1   Web site flowchart.

Start early. Avoid waiting to the last moment to develop and deploy a Web site (e.g., not deploying until the start of the execution phase). Do so as soon as possible so it becomes an integral part for providing information on a project.

Determine the purpose. What are the reasons for the Web site? Serving as a medium to distribute information? Providing visibility of results? Failure to determine the purpose of the site can result in it becoming a "garbage can" of data. The purpose will also determine the structure and logical flow of a site.

Determine the audience. This guideline has a close relationship with determining the purpose. By knowing the audience, project managers can tailor and organize the content to satisfy the needs of the audience.

Determine the content. The content can vary tremendously based upon who the stakeholders are and their respective requirements. These requirements will determine the quality, content, and degree of detail that they or others can expect to access. Nevertheless, it is possible to ascertain the types of different data and information to be made available on a project Web site. These types include:

- "S" curves (cost, schedule, technical)
- Earned value charts (e.g., SPI and CPI tracking and monitoring)
- Estimates (e.g., summary)
- Flowcharts
- Histograms (by specific category)
- Inventory lists
- Links
- Maps
- Network diagram (high level)
- Organization chart
- Policies and procedures
- Project announcement
- Project charter
- Quality charts (e.g., Pareto charts, scatter grams)
- Reference documentation
- Reports (at different levels of summary)
- Responsibility assignment matrices
- Risk charts
- Schedules (multitier)
- Statement of work
- Statistics (e.g., technical)
- Work breakdown structure (e.g., tree diagram)

Determine the structure and logical flow. Structure means that project managers must determine the pages and their content, often displayed in a hierarchy chart (Figure 9.2). Logical flow means determining movement from one page to another. The goal is to provide stakeholders with an appropriate view that helps them to

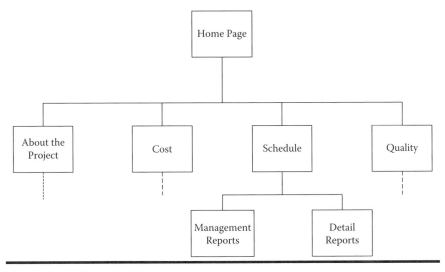

Figure 9.2   Hierarchy chart.

fulfill their needs quickly. Structure and logical flow are instrumental in satisfying access requirements for data and information.

Use good design principles. The bottom line is that pages should present data and information concisely and clearly. Pages should appear uncluttered, and both structure and content should be modular. On each page, content should be clearly identifiable, contain good grammar and spelling, and facilitate usage. Through early assignment of responsibilities and establishing configuration control practices, a site will become an asset rather than an administrative nightmare so that good design principles are followed throughout the life cycle of a project.

Some additional basics of good design heuristics to consider when developing a project Web site are:

- Avoid excessive navigation and hypertext links.
- Emphasize the need to maximize download speeds.
- Employ color in a meaningful way.
- Enable visitors to find, rather than search for, data and information.
- Keep links current.
- Minimize the amount of graphics, such as icons and pictures.
- Modularize the layout.
- Offer a search capability.
- Prefer the specific to the general.
- Provide a site map.
- Standardize the page layout.
- Use consistent terminology.
- Use the least amount of text and maximize the degree of white space.

Obtain tools. Developing and deploying a Web site on an intranet is a relatively easy endeavor after sketching the layout of the content. Basically, project managers need Web development software and server space. Of course, the degree of sophistication will decide whether the expertise of a Webmaster and programmer are necessary. If they want to provide sophisticated functionality, such as restricting access to certain data or automating the movement of data from one server to another, then more sophisticated expertise may be necessary.

Deploy the Web site. Technically, deploying a site is easy. Having adequate server space and the necessary Web application, such as Sharepoint, ProjectLink, or Front-Page, are all that is needed. However, that is only one part of the deployment.

The other part is communicating to all the stakeholders that the Web site is available. Project managers can accomplish that through e-mails announcing the site's existence at meetings and requesting that team members use the Web site to communicate and share information.

Set up an update schedule. Although project managers may find themselves needing to post data and information on an ad hoc basis to a Web site, they might find it best to establish a specific time (e.g., every Tuesday at 4 p.m.) to post new material via a Webmaster. This approach will help them to ensure better currency and relevancy of data and information. Conducting a periodic review of the overall Web site would also help in determining the relevancy of content (e.g., looking at access and usage statistics).

Encourage use of the Web site. Although a project may have the "best" site in the world, stakeholder visits may be rare. The best ways to ensure site usage is to use the site to post the most important data and information. In addition, upon updating the content, notify everyone about the update; an e-mail with a set distribution list works effectively in this respect. Another way to ensure usage is to access the relevant data and information on the Web site during meetings, such as project reviews and stand ups.

Minimizing response times, through optimization and configuration of the network, too, can have a great impact on whether people will use the Web site. Project managers, therefore, should strive to have team members who possess machines with sufficient random access memory (RAM) and faster central processor units (CPUs).

Control updates. A Web site can contain too much data and information, adding rather than lessening confusion. If people have carte blanche to update a site, the project manager will not only lose configuration control but see confusion develop over what data and information are relevant and accurate. The best alternatives are to place a site under strict configuration control (e.g., restrict changes to designated people) and to grant review and approval authority over selected categories of data and information to selected people (e.g., a project manager or Webmaster).

Sharing and Visibility

A project Web site, next to a communications management plan itself, is a project manager's most important tool for communications. It provides a vehicle for sharing data and information. It also provides an effective way to give visibility to progress and areas that need improvement. Once something is on a Web site people find it very difficult to restrict or hide data and information.

Getting Started Checklist		Yes	No
Questions			
1.	When developing, deploying, and maintaining a Web site for a project, do you perform these steps:		
	Determine audience		
	Determine purpose		
	Determine content		
	Determine structure		
	Determine logical flow		
	Use good design principles		
	Obtain tools		
	Deploy the site		
	Set up an update schedule		
	Encourage the use of the site		
	Control updates		
2.	When determining content for the Web site, do you consider items like:		
	"S" curves (cost, schedule, technical)		
	Earned value charts (e.g., SPI and CPI tracking and monitoring)		
	Estimates (e.g., summary)		
	Flowcharts		
	Histograms (by specific category)		
	Inventory lists		
	Links		
	Maps		
	Network diagram (high level)		
	Organization chart		
	Policies and procedures		
	Project announcement		

Getting Started Checklist (Continued)		
Questions	*Yes*	*No*
Project charter		
Quality charts (e.g., Pareto charts, scatter grams)		
Reference documentation		
Reports (at different levels of summary)		
Responsibility assignment matrices		
Risk charts		
Schedules (multitier)		
Statement of work		
Statistics (e.g., technical)		
Work breakdown structure (e.g., tree diagram)		

Chapter 10

Building War Rooms

A war, or control, room is a facility that provides stakeholders with a location to communicate and collaborate. More often than not, a war room is for people who are physically present on a project, albeit that may not always be true; some members may work virtually.

PMIS Contributions

As with the project Web site, a PMIS can provide material for what appears on the walls. The same challenges exist. The materials on the walls should match what is in the PMIS and a need may exist to limit visibility of materials to ensure the protection of proprietary data and information.

Many Pluses

A war room is similar to a command center in the military. It functions as a hub, or central facility, for managing a campaign, in this case a project. As such, it offers several advantages, including:

- Boosting morale by collocating people
- Offering a convenient work area
- Providing a convenient meeting place for regular and ad hoc meetings
- Providing visibility of performance
- Serving as a communications center

Key Steps

A war room, if it is to effectively contribute to a project, must be well planned and organized. To ensure that contributions become a reality, follow these guidelines (Figure 10.1).

First, consider the audience. The audience will determine how to best use the room and display its contents. For management the content will be different for the team members, often a reflection of detail and display. Customers invited to the room will also influence content and its display.

Second, sketch the layout in advance by involving stakeholders to determine content and display. For example, consider displaying certain material as charts, diagrams, and tabular reports. Also, display information in a specific sequence. The primary reason for sketching the layout is to obtain consensus over content, format, relevance, and detail that will appear in the room. Content often includes these topics:

- "S" curves (cost, schedule, technical)
- Earned value charts (e.g., SPI and CPI tracking and monitoring)
- Estimates (e.g., summary)
- Flowcharts
- Histograms (by specific category)
- Inventory lists
- Maps
- Network diagram (high level)
- Organization chart
- Policies and procedures
- Project announcement
- Project charter
- Quality charts (e.g., Pareto charts, scatter grams)

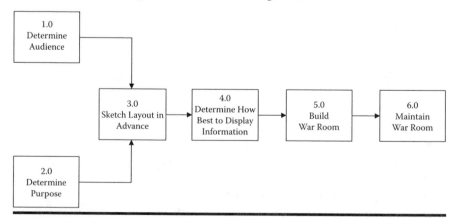

Figure 10.1   War room flowchart.

- Reference documentation
- Reports (at different levels of summary)
- Responsibility assignment matrices
- Risk charts
- Schedules (multitier)
- Statement of work
- Statistics (e.g., technical)
- Work breakdown structure (e.g., tree)

Third, determine how to best display information (Figures 10.2, 10.3, and 10.4). In some cases, charts, diagrams, and other reports may be printed on a plotter. In other cases, the information may be displayed best using electronic equipment on a screen. If needing electronic equipment and supplies, they will likely include:

- Assorted supplies, including pens, easel pads, and notepads
- Bridge lines
- Easel pad stands
- Microcomputers with sufficient drop lines
- Projector equipment
- Seating and a conference tables
- White boards

Fourth, determine the purpose. This step is usually performed jointly with the audience. A war room could have one or more purposes. These purposes could be to:

- Provide a work area
- Give visibility to work performed
- Hold ad hoc and regularly scheduled meetings (e.g., status reviews)
- Serve as a telecommunications and video conferencing center
- Impress visitors (e.g., VIPs)

Fifth, build the war room. This step requires considerable forethought, although it is sometimes overlooked. Building the war room requires making decisions about the quality and quantity of content, the time and effort to expend for construction and maintenance, the arrangement of seating, the type of equipment, type and amount of supplies, and much more. The key to building a control room is thinking about it prior to its actual construction. Thinking about what to provide and how to lay it out in advance will reduce the time to build it and minimize the costs resulting from rework.

Sixth, maintain the war room. If used extensively, a war room can become very disorganized and messy (e.g., leftover snacks), which makes using such a room quite uncomfortable and impacts productivity.

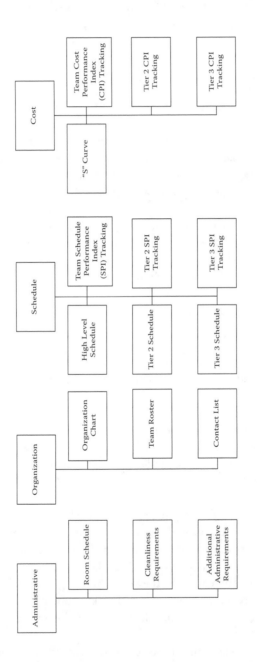

Figure 10.2 War room wall number 1.

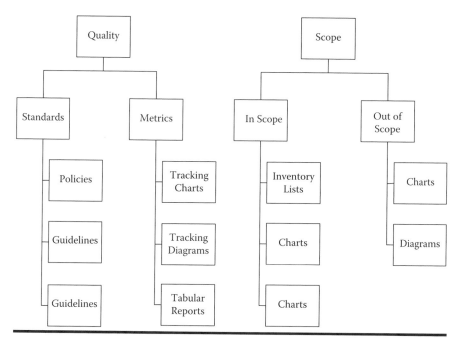

Figure 10.3   War room wall number 2.

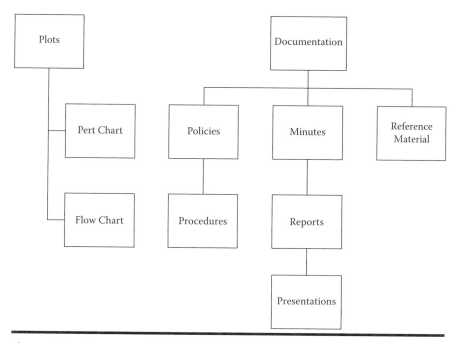

Figure 10.4   War room wall number 3.

An additional point about maintenance is the content. Data and information on the walls must be kept current if people are expected to use the room as a communications center and a work room. Out-of-date material can result in obviating the entire purpose of the room; essentially, it becomes nothing more than another conference room.

Challenges

A war room presents several challenges to address if it is to prove useful to a project.

Keeping the war room current. The contents of the wall must be updated so that people will find the material relevant and useful during discussions. Failure to keep the material current turns the displays into fancy wallpaper consisting of pretty pictures and charts. Some of the more flagrant examples of not keeping the room current include not placing on the walls the latest information, such as scheduling and cost charts and reports; rosters; and risk charts.

Displaying the content of the war room consistently and logically for the purposes of access and visibility. For example, all of the charts and diagrams should have a consistent layout for easy referencing and readability. Closely allied to this point is that you should have the material on the wall well organized into logical groupings that enable easy access and will be easily followed from one topic to the next (e.g., topics covered at a project review meeting). Too often, people place diagrams, charts, and reports haphazardly on the walls. Naturally, there is not a logical flow to the content. Not only do stakeholders have difficulty in following the logic behind the material being shown but they may have to also hunt for the specific diagram, chart, or report that they need.

Ensuring that the material on the walls is useful to the people. Populating the walls with superfluous material not only adds clutter but may also confuse people and "squeeze out" more important information. A common practice is to place something on the wall to cover a blank spot or display something that looks nice but is not very impressive. The problem with this action is that it detracts from the important information on the wall, causes people to have to hunt for what they want, and occupies space that could be useful in the future.

Keeping the war room clean. Because stakeholders may frequent the room, a tendency exists for letting the next group of people "deal with the mess." The clutter can get overwhelming. Project managers should stress that the cleanliness of the room is a shared responsibility. As a side note, many companies have rules for meetings listed on posters in war rooms. A good practice is to have listed as one of the rules to clean the room at the end of each meeting. These rooms can get quite littered, especially if they serve as much a work room as they do a communications center. Sometimes, the displays on the wall, such as output from plotters, can fall off the wall and lie on the floor behind a chair, or be tossed onto a table and stay there for days. A little preventive maintenance can go a long way in keeping a control room clean.

Ensuring that the room has working equipment and available supplies. If a war room is ill equipped or has a supply shortage, the quality of the meetings will likely be impacted. Nothing disrupts a meeting more than when equipment fails or people must hunt for supplies. Some common problems include not having enough markers for white boards, push pins to put diagrams on walls, and pencils and pens to mark up displays. Some common equipment problems include not having enough drops for laptops, extension cords or outlets, and bulbs for projectors.

Controlling access. Post a schedule for its use outside of the entrance door or reflect its usage in meeting schedule software, such as Microsoft Outlook. People should have access to the schedule so that people do not arrive and interrupt an ongoing session or cause needless power struggles over who has access to the room. A war room should not, ironically, actually look like a war zone. To serve stakeholders well, it requires the utmost attention to provide the right information in the right amount in the right format to the right people.

The bottom line is that a war room is an asset for planning, executing, and controlling a project. That requires considering a number of factors, including appearance, costs (for set up and maintenance), size, and layout.

Valuable Asset

Some people see a control room as a waste of space. They are correct if the rooms lack cleanliness, organization, and relevant data and information. If project managers and other stakeholders view a control room as an asset then the likelihood of use will grow both as a communications tool, a way to improve morale, and, ultimately, a center of increased productivity.

Getting Started Checklist		
Questions	*Yes*	*No*
1. When building and maintaining a war room, do you:		
Determine the audience?		
Determine the purpose?		
Sketch the layout in advance?		
Determine how to best display information?		
Build a war room?		
Maintain a war room?		
2. To determine the content of the war room, do you consider:		
Earned value charts (e.g., SPI and CPI tracking and monitoring)?		
Estimates (e.g., summary)?		
Flowcharts?		
Histograms (by specific category)?		
Inventory lists?		
Maps?		
Network diagram (high level)?		
Organization chart?		
Policies and procedures?		
Project announcement?		
Project charter?		
Quality charts (e.g., Pareto charts, scatter grams)?		
Reference documentation?		
Reports (at different levels of summary)?		
Responsibility assignment matrices?		
Risk charts?		
Schedules (multitier)?		
"S" curves (cost, schedule, or technical)?		
Statement of work?		
Statistics (e.g., technical)?		
Work breakdown structure (e.g., tree)?		
3. For equipment and supplies, do you consider:		
Assorted supplies, including pens, easel pads, and notepads?		
Bridge lines?		
Easel pad stands?		

Getting Started Checklist (Continued)			
Questions		*Yes*	*No*
	Microcomputers with sufficient drop lines?		
	Projector equipment?		
	Seating and conference tables?		
	White boards?		
4.	Have you considered how to overcome challenges like:		
	Controlling access?		
	Displaying the content of the war room consistently and logically for the purposes of access and visibility?		
	Ensuring that the material on the walls is useful?		
	Ensuring that the room has working equipment and available supplies?		
	Keeping the room current?		
	Keeping the war room clean?		
5.	Have you identified the purposes of the war room, for instance, should it:		
	Give visibility to work performed?		
	Allow holding of ad hoc and regularly scheduled meetings (e.g., status reviews)?		
	Impress visitors (e.g., VIPs)?		
	Provide a work area?		
	Serve as a telecommunications and video conferencing center?		

Chapter 11

The Key to Effective Leadership

Project managers communicate much of their time and, ironically, often communicate poorly. By implementing a project management information system, or PMIS, they lay the groundwork for becoming effective communicators on their projects.

PMIS Requires Good Data

The PMIS allows them to manage their most important resource—data—in a manner that allows them to execute seven basic communications processes:

- Applying active and effective listening
- Preparing a communications management plan and establishing an issues management process
- Drafting and publishing documentation
- Conducting meetings
- Giving effective presentations
- Developing and deploying a Web site
- Building war rooms

Many project managers, however, treat the idea of a PMIS too casually. They fall into the trap of thinking that the management of data will evolve into something that they can handle as a project proceeds through the life cycle. Unfortunately, this belief leads to considerable dysfunction on a project: miscommunication, confusion, rework, frustration, and impatience, just to name a few problems. At the core of these and other dysfunctions is poor communications.

The reality is that project managers can avoid these and other problems by developing and deploying an integrated system that turns data into information for all stakeholders on a project. The information generated by the PMIS enables project managers to become better listeners and better presenters, and implement media that serves everyone's interests.

Too much of the "I thought you knew what I knew" exists on projects. People, especially project managers, begin to operate on assumptions that frequently turn out incorrect. When that happens, confidence begins to wane in the project managers and in the media that they employ on projects. As often the case, when the confidence goes, so does the credibility.

PM Disciplines Not Enough

Many project managers think that by merely putting good project management disciplines in place will solve the issue and allow them to be good communicators. They are mistaken. All that happens is project managers employ disciplines that generate information that no one can use because of bad data. Discipline with unreliable information leads to bad decisions and negative results. It's akin to giving a painter high tech tools to paint a house. The problem is that if the paint itself is of poor quality and begins to run or fade after the first storm, the tools make very little difference.

Leadership

It is interesting to note that one of the key characteristics of effective leadership is the ability to communicate. Using that as the premise, project managers who become adroit as communicators will likely become, if they are not already, effective leaders. Interesting to note, too, is that leadership, like communications, is in short supply on projects. Yet, both are needed in every phase of the project life cycle.

Many times, project managers cry over the fact that they lack power. What they fail to realize is that they have an instrument of power available to them. The PMIS is that instrument, and it is used to collect data to generate the life blood of any organization, in general, and any project, in particular, which provides information.

It was Socrates who wrote that knowledge is power, and that remains true today with one exception. Information is power in the contemporary environment, and project managers who have the information they need to manage their projects wield power by the fact that information gives them necessary knowledge.

References

Books

Armstrong, Thomas. *Seven Kinds of Smarts: Identifying and Developing Your Many Intelligences.* New York: Plume, 1993.

Baker, Ernst. Communications/Negotiation Techniques That Work! 2004 PMI Global Congress Proceedings. Newtown Square: Project Management Institute, 2004.

Barker, Joel A. *Paradigms.* New York: Harper Business, 1993.

Barkley, Bruce T. and Saylor, James H. *Customer-Driven Project Management: Building Quality in Project Processes.* New York: McGraw-Hill, 2001.

Bolton, Robert. *People Skills.* New York: Touchstone, 1986.

Boredelon, Jeanette. Be a Positive PM Change Agent. 2004 PMI Global Congress Proceedings. Newtown Square: Project Management Institute, 2004.

Bramsom, Robert M. *Coping with Difficult People.* New York: Dell, 1981.

Brassard, Michael. *The Memory Jogger Plus+: Featuring the Seven Management and Planning Tools.* Methuen, MA: GOAL/QPC, 1989.

Briner, Wendy; Geddes, Michael; and Hastings, Colin. *Project Leadership.* Aldershot, England: Gower, 1990.

Buzan, Tony. *Use Both Sides of Your Brain.* New York: E. P. Dutton, 1983.

Carnell, Angie and Sikes, Sharon. Dog Guides, Interpreters and You. 2004 PMI Global Congress Proceedings. Newtown Square: Project Management Institute, 2004.

Curlee, Wanda and Gordon, Robert. Leading through Conflict in a Virtual Team. 2004 PMI Global Congress Proceedings. Newtown Square: Project Management Institute, 2004.

De Bono, Edward. *Six Thinking Hats.* Boston, MA: Little Brown, 1985.

Dekkers, Carol. Maximize Project Success: Get a Communications Skills Tune-Up. 2004 PMI Global Congress Proceedings. Newtown Square: Project Management Institute, 2004.

Dimov, Peter. Leadership: When Management Is Not Enough. 2004 PMI Global Congress Proceedings. Newtown Square: Project Management Institute, 2004.

Dorner, Dietrich. *The Logic of Failure: Recognizing and Avoiding Error in Complex Situations.* Cambridge, MA: Metropolitan Books, 1996.

Englund, Randall R. Leading with Power. 2004 PMI Global Congress Proceedings. Newtown Square: Project Management Institute, 2004. Newtown Square: Project Management Institute, 2004.

Fast, Julius. *Body Language: The Essential Secrets of Non-Verbal Communications.* New York: MJF Books, 1970.

Ferraro, Jack P. Do You Trust That Project Manager in the Mirror? 2004 PMI Global Congress Proceedings. Newtown Square: Project Management Institute, 2004.

Fox, William M. *Effective Group Problem Solving.* San Francisco, CA: Jossey-Bass Publishers, 1990.

Gardner, Howard. *Frames of Mind: The Theory of Multiple Intelligences.* New York: Basic Books, 1983.

Gardner, Howard. *Multiple Intelligences: The Theory in Practice.* New York: Basic Books, 1993.

Gebelein, Susan H. et al. *Successful Manager's Handbook: Development Suggestions for Today's Manager.* USA: Personnel Decisions International, 2000.

Glass, Robert L. *Software Communication Skills.* Englewood Cliffs, NJ: Prentice Hall, 1988.

Hartman, Taylor. *The Color Code.* New York: Fireside Books, 1998.

Hayes, Brigitte. When the Project Has Many Faces in Many Places: Software Tools for the Distributed Team. 2004 PMI Global Congress Proceedings. Newtown Square: Project Management Institute, 2004.

Herrmann, Ned. *The Whole Brain Book.* New York: McGraw-Hill, 1996.

Holm, James N. *Productive Speaking for Business and the Professions.* Boston: Allyn & Bacon, 1967.

Infane, Dominic A., Rancer, Andrew S., and Womack, Deanna F. *Building Communication Theory.* Prospect Heights, IL: Waveland Press, 1997.

Karraass, Chester L. *The Negotiating Game.* New York: Thomas Y. Crowell Co., 1970.

Keirsey, David and Bates, Marilyn. *Please Understand Me.* Del Mar, CA: Prometheus Nemesis, 1984.

Kerzner, Harold. *Project Management: A Systems Approach to Planning, Scheduling, and Controlling.* New York: Van Nostrand Reinhold, 1995.

Kliem, Ralph L. and Anderson, Harris B. *The Organizational Engineering Approach to Project Management.* Boca Raton, FL: St. Lucie Press, 2003.

Kliem, Ralph L. and Ludin, Irwin S. *Stand and Deliver: The Fine Art of Presentation.* Aldershot, England: Gower, 1995.

Kliem, Ralph L. and Ludin, Irwin S. *Tools and Tips for Today's Project Manager.* Newtown Square, PA: Project Management Institute, 1999.

Kliem, Ralph L. *Leading High Performance Projects.* Boca Raton, FL: J. Ross Publishing, 2004.

Kliem, Ralph L. *The Project Manager's Emergency Kit.* Boca Raton, FL: St. Lucie Press, 2003.

Kliem, Ralph L., Ludin, Irwin S., and Robertson, Ken L. *Project Management Methodology: A Practical Guide for the Next Millennium.* New York: Marcel Dekker, 1997.

Kluge, Jurgen; Stein, Wolfram; and Licht, Thomas. *Knowledge Unplugged.* New York: Palgrave, 2001.

Kuhn, Thomas. *The Structure of Scientific Revolutions.* Chicago, IL: University of Chicago Press, 1970.

Levin, Ginger and Rad, Parvic. Requirements for Effective Project Communications: Differences and Similarities in Virtual and Traditional Project Environments. 2004 PMI Global Congress Proceedings. Newtown Square: Project Management Institute, 2004.

Lewis, James P. *Project Leadership.* New York: McGraw-Hill, 2003.

Lewis, James P. *Project Planning, Scheduling and Control,* 3rd ed., New York: McGraw-Hill, 2000.

Lewis, James P. *The Project Manager's Desk Reference: A Comprehensive Guide to Project Planning, Scheduling, Evaluation, Control, and Systems.* Chicago, IL: Irwin Professional Publishing, 1995.

Lipnack, Jessica and Stamps, Jeffrey. *Virtual Teams: People Working across Boundaries with Technology,* 2nd ed., New York: John Wiley, 2000.

Mulcahy, Rita. *PMP Prep Exam: A Course in a Book,* 4th ed., RMC Publications, 2002.

Newell, Michael W. *Preparing for the Project Management Professional (PMP) Certification Exam.* New York: AMACOM, 2001.

Nierenberg, Gerard I. and Calero, Henry H. *MetaTalk: How to Uncover the Hidden Meanings in What People Say.* New York: Simon & Schuster, 1981.

Nierenberg, Gerard I. *The Art of Negotiating.* New York: Cornerstone Library, 1968.

Nutt, Paul C. *Why Decisions Fail.* San Francisco, CA: Berrett-Koehler, 2002.

Palmer, Helen. *The Enneagram: Understanding Yourself and the Others in Your Life.*

People, David A. *Presentations Plus.* New York: John Wiley, 1988.

Plotnik, Arthur. *The Elements of Editing: A Modern Guide for Editors & Journalists.* New York: MacMillan, 1982.

Proceedings of the PMI Research Conference 2002. Newton Square, PA: Project Management Institute, 2002.

Project Management Institute. A *Guide to the Project Management Body of Knowledge.* 3rd ed., Newtown Square, PA: Project Management Institute, 2004.

Rabb, Margaret Y. *The Presentation Design Book.* Chapel Hill, NC: Ventana Press, 1993.

Ress, Jay. Proactive Communication for Project Managers. 2004 PMI Global Congress Proceedings. Newtown Square: Project Management Institute, 2004.

Riso, Don R. *Personality Types: Using the Enneagram for Self-Discovery.* Boston, MA: Houghton-Mifflin, 1997.

Ronneberg, Harald. Perceptions of Project Team Performance. 2004 PMI Global Congress Proceedings. Newtown Square: Project Management Institute, 2004.

Ross, Russell C. *Speak with Ease.* 2nd ed., New York: Funk and Wagnalls, 1961.

Rotondo, Jennifer and Rotondo, Mike Jr. *Presentation Skills for Managers.* New York: McGraw-Hill, 2002.

Russo, Edward J. and Shoemaker, Paul J. *Decision Traps: The Ten Barriers to Brilliant Decision-Making and How to Overcome Them.* New York: Simon & Schuster, 1989.

Shertzer, Margaret. *The Elements of Grammar.* New York: MacMillan, 1986.

Strunk, William, Jr. and White, E. B., *The Elements of Style,* 3rd ed., New York: MacMillan, 1979.

Thomas, Janice; Mengel, Thomas; and Andres Natale. Surfing on the Edge of Chaos. 2004 PMI Global Congress Proceedings. Newtown Square: Project Management Institute, 2004.

Tubbs, Stewart and Moss, Sylvia. *Human Communication.* 8th ed., Boston, MA: McGraw-Hill, 2000.

Verma, Vijay K. *Human Resource Skills for the Project Manager.* Newtown Square, PA: Project Management Institute, 1996.

Verzuh, Eric. Building the Problem Solving Machine: Team Building Guidelines for Project Managers. 2004 PMI Global Congress Proceedings. Newtown Square: Project Management Institute, 2004.

Verzuh, Eric. *The Fast Forward MBA in Project Management,* 2nd ed., Hoboken, NJ: John Wiley, 2005.

Verzuh, Eric. *The Portable MBA in Project Management.* Hoboken, NJ: John Wiley, 2003.

Whitten, Neal. *Managing Software Development Projects.* New York: John Wiley, 1990.

Williams, Linda V. *Teaching for the Two-Sided Brain.* New York: Simon & Schuster, 1983.

Wonder, Jacquelyn and Donovan, Priscilla. *Whole Brain Thinking.* New York: Ballantine Books, 1984.

Wurman, Richard S. *Information Anxiety: What to Do When Information Doesn't Tell What You Need to Know.* New York: Bantam Books, 1989.

Zeitoun, Al. Selling the "Project Management Message" to Enable Organizational Excellence. 2004 PMI Global Congress Proceedings. Newtown Square: Project Management Institute, 2004.

Articles

Abramson, Craig. Improve Your Analysis Capabilities. *What Works.* Vol. 19.

Ambler, Scott W. Requirements Wisdom. *Software Development.* October 2005.

Baldwin, Howard. Managing Virtual Teams. *Global Services.* August 2006.

Barth, Steve. The Evolution of Desktop Search: Good News for the Knowledge Worker. *KM World.* February 2005.

Bazerman, Max H. How Did I Miss That? *Computerworld.* January 9, 2006.

Beal, Barney. Diving into Dashboards. *CIO Decisions.* June 2006.

Becker, Bob. Data Stewardship 101: First Step to Quality and Consistency. *Intelligent Enterprise. June 2006.*

Bontempo, Charles and Zagelow. George. The IBM Data Warehouse Architecture. *Communications of the ACM.* September 1998.

Brandel, Mary. The New Project Manager. *Computerworld.* April 10, 2006.

Brath, Richard and Peters, Mike. Information Visualization for Business: Past & Future. *Data Management Review.* January 2005.

Buytendijk, Frank. Quality Control: How to Respond to "Just Give Me a Dashboard!" *Business Performance Management.* September 2005.

Chandras, Rajan. EII: Information on Demand. *Intelligent Enterprise.* February 2005.

Christensen, Matt. Avoiding Common Dashboard Pitfalls. *Data Management Review.* November 2006.

Communication Is Key to Success. *Journal of Accountancy.* March 2005.

Cramm, Susan. The Heart of Persuasion. *CIO.* July 1, 2005.

Creese, Guy. Information Scarcity to Information Overload. *Data Management Review.* January 2007.

Dalton, Aaron. Human Capital. *PM Network.* August 2006.

Demarest, George. Zen and the Art of Information. *Oracle Magazine.* March/April 2005.

Dignan, Larry. Less Is Better. *Baseline Magazine.* May 2005.

Dignan, Larry. Habit Forming: Use These 11 Simple Rules to Build Your Information Management Prowess. *Baseline Magazine.* October 2004.

Dravis, Frank. Data Quality: Horizontal or Vertical? *Data Management Review.* August 2006.

Drucker, Peter F. The Next Information Revolution. *Forbes ASAP.* August 24, 1998.

Dunn, Jeff. Power-Start Your Speech Prep. *The Toastmaster.* August 2005.

Eckerson, Wayne W. See It Coming. *Intelligent Enterprise.* February 2006.

Eckerson, Wayne W. Data Quality and the Bottom Line. *Application Development Trends.* May 2002.

Eckerson, Wayne W. Analytic Apps Add New Logic to Dashboards. *Application Development Trends.* January 2005.

Eckerson, Wayne W. Data Profiling: A Tool Worth Buying (Really!). *Data Management Review.* June 2004.

Edwards, John. Picture This. *CFO.* November 2005.

Elliott, Timo and Cunningham, Darren. The Burden of Trusted Information. *Data Management Review.* June 2005.

English, Larry P. IQ and Muda: Information Quality Eliminates Waste. *Data Management Review.* September 2005.

English, Larry P. The 14 Points of Information Quality Transformation. *Data Management Review.* November 2006.

English, Larry P. The Essentials of Information Quality Management. *Data Management Review.* September 2002.

Ericson, Jim. Investing in Information. *Data Management Review.* September 2006.

Erlanger, Leon. Information from Start to Finish. *Infoworld.* June 6, 2005.

Essex, David E. Anytime Anywhere. *PM Network.* November 2006.

Few, Stephen. Boxes of Insight. *Data Management Review.* August 2005.

Few, Stephen. Common Mistakes in Data Representation. *Intelligent Enterprise.* August 7, 2004.

Few, Stephen. Creative Visualization: Best in Show. *Data Management Review.* October 2005.

Few, Stephen. Data Presentation: Tapping the Power of Visual Presentation. *Intelligent Enterprise.* September 4, 2004.

Few, Stephen. Eenie, Meenie, Minie, Moe: Selecting the Right Graph for Your Message. *Intelligent Enterprise.* September 18, 2004.

Few, Stephen. Elegance through Simplicity. *Intelligent Enterprise.* October 16, 2004.

Few, Stephen. Grid Lines in Graphs Are Rarely Useful. *Data Management Review.* February 2005.

Few, Stephen. Intelligent Dashboard Design. *Data Management Review.* September 2005.

Few, Stephen. Quantitative vs. categorical Data. *Data Management Review.* April 2005.

Few, Stephen. Uses and Misuses of Color. *Data Management Review.* November 2005.

Few, Stephen. Visualizing Multidimensional Data through Time. *Data Management Review.* July 2005.

Fogarty, Kevin. Learn to Manage Data, Not Crises. *Computerworld.* April 15, 2002.

Fretty, Peter. Why Do Projects Really Fail? *PM Network.* March 2006.

Furey, Tim. Data Warehouse Project Management. *Data Management Review.* May 2005.

Gale, Sarah F. Clear Channels. *PM Network.* September 2005.

Gardner, Stephen R. Building the Data Warehouse. *Communications of the ACM.* September 1998.

Geiger, Jonathan. Ensuring Data Quality. *Data Management Review.* January 2007.

Geiger, Jonathan. Managing the Total Cost of Ownership. *Data Management Review.* June 2006.

Ghiossi, Rich. Data Aggregation: Seven Key Criteria to an Effective Aggregation Solution. *What Works.* Vol. 19.

Gilhooly, Kym. Dirty Data Blights the Bottom Line. *Computerworld.* November 7, 2005.

Gill, Philip J. On the Trail of Knowledge. *Knowledge Management.* January 2001.

Gonzales, Michael L. The Architecture of Enterprise Data Quality. *Intelligent Enterprise.* June 1, 2004.

Grimes, Seth. Seeing the Connection. *Intelligent Enterprise.* August 7, 2004.

Grimes, Seth. Simultaneous Equation Models. *Intelligent Enterprise.* February 16, 2001.

Gruman, Galen. The Right Information, Right Now. *Infoworld.* October 11, 2004.

Hall, Mark. Seeding for Data Growth. *Computerworld.* April 15, 2002.

Halper, Mark. Welcome to 21st Century Data. *Forbes ASAP.* April 8, 1996.

Haughey, Tom. Is Dimensional Modeling One of the Great Con Jobs in Data Management History? (Part 1). *Data Management Review.* March 2004.

Hildebrand, Carol. The Eyes Have It. *PM Network.* May 2006.

Holzschlag, Molly E. Satisfying Customers with Color, Shape, and Type. *Web Techniques.* November 1999.

Hooke, Mary V. Maximize Performance with Indexes. *Visual Basic Programming Journal.* October 1999.

Hot Button. *PM Network.* October 2006.

Iervolino, Chris. Don't Forget the Data: Keeping the Right Focus in Consolidation and Reporting. *Business Performance Management.* June 2004.

Imhoff, Claudia and Sousa, Ryan. Information Ecosystem (Part 2). *Data Management Review.* February 1997.

Imhoff, Claudia and Sousa, Ryan. Information Ecosystem (Part 3). *Data Management Review.* March 1997.

Imhoff, Claudia and Sousa, Ryan. Information Ecosystem (Part 4). *Data Management Review.* April 1997.

Imhoff, Claudia and Sousa, Ryan. Information Ecosystem (Part 5). *Data Management Review.* May 1997.

Imhoff, Claudia. Lessons from the Farm: Managing the Data Delivery Process. *Data Management Review.* November 2004.

Inside Information. *Smart Business Magazine.* June 2002.

In Trouble, *PM Network.* September 2006.

Jedd, Marcia. Project Rescue. *PM Network.* January 2006.

Kapur, Gopal K. 4 key Talking Points for Good Communication. *CIO Decisions.* September 2006.

Kelly, David A. Tame Your Content. *Oracle Magazine.* March/April 2005.

King, Eric A. How to Buy Data Mining. *Data Management Review.* October 2005.

Laurent, William. The Case for Data Stewardship. *Data Management Review.* February 2005.

Leading Edge. *PM Network.* June 2006.

Linder, Jane and Phelps, Drew. Call to Action. *CIO.* April 1, 2000.

Lindquist, Christopher. Fixing the Requirements Mess. *CIO.* November 15, 2005.

Logue, Ann C. Dysfunction Junction. *PM Network.* August 2006.

Losey, Rand. Enterprise Data Architecture: Who Needs It? *Data Management Review.* January 2004.

Loshin, David. Develop Information Quality Metrics. *Data Management Review.* May 2005.

Loshin, David. Information Flow Modeling. *Data Management Review.* April 2003.

Loshin, David. Information Synergy. *Data Management Review.* January 2005.

Loshin, David. Intelligent Information Processing. *Data Management Review.* July 2001.

Madsen, Mark. Data As It Happens. *Intelligent Enterprise.* May 31, 2003.

Marco, David. Data Assurance Road Map (Part 1). *Data Management Review.* December 2004.

Marco, David. Data Assurance Road Map (Part 2). *Data Management Review.* January 2005.

Marinos, George. The Information Supply Chain. *Data Management Review.* April 2005.

McGee, Marianne K. The Useless Hunt for Data. *Information Week.* January 8, 2007.

McGilvray, Danette. Data Governance: A Necessity in an Integrated Information World. *Data Management Review.* December 2006.

Mearian, Lucas. The 100-Year Archive Dilemma. *Computerworld.* July 25, 2005.

Mentrup, Lois. Social Network. *PM Network.* August 2006.

Mishra, Sanjay. Making Data Flow. *Oracle Magazine.* November/December 2004.

Mok, Clement and Zauderer, Vic. Timeless Principles of Design. *Web Techniques.* April 1997.

Nance-Nash, Sheryl. Everybody's a Critic. *PM Network.* October 2006.

Nash, Kim S. Merging Data Silos. *Computerworld.* April 15, 2002.

Newell, Allen. The Knowledge Level. *AI Magazine.* Summer 1981.

Norris, David. The End of Information Overload. Data *Management Review.* September 2005.

Ohlson, Kathleen. A View to the Thrill of Data. *Application Development Trends.* August 2005.

Orr, Ken. Data Quality and Systems Theory. *Communications of the ACM.* February 1998.

Palluzi, Richard. Drowning in Data. *Intech.* September 2006.

Panakal, Denny and Medley, Michelle. The Global Project Management Challenge. *Dr. Dobb's Journal.* February 2007.

Pratt, Mary. Meeting of Minds. *Computerworld.* September 26, 2005.

Prewitt, Edward. Why IT Leaders Fail. *CIO.* August 1, 2005.

Redman, Thomas C. The Impact of Poor Data Quality on the Typical Enterprise. *Communications of the ACM.* February 1998.

Redmand, Thomas C. Data: An Unfolding Quality Disaster. *Data Management Review.* August 2004.

Robb, Drew. Global Workgroups. *Computerworld.* August 15, 2005.

Roiter, Neil. That Sinking Feeling…Before You Lose Something Precious, Govern Your Data. *Information Security.* October 2006.

Seeing into the Future. *PM Network.* December 2006.

Sen, Aren and Jacob, Varghese S. Industrial Strength Data Warehousing. *Communications of the ACM.* September 1998.

Settle-Murphy, Nancy and Thornton, Caroline. Facilitating Your Way to Project Success. *Information Strategy: The Executive's Journal.* Spring 1999.

Shah, Faisal. Data Integration Techniques for reliable Information Delivery. *Data Management Review.* November 2005.

Shenk, David. Why You Feel the Way You Do. *Inc.* January 1999.

Shirky, Clay. Getting Out from Under. *Fortune.* March 20, 2006.

Silverston, Len. Universal Data Models and Patterns. *Data Management Review.* November 2005.

Simons, Tad. Does PowerPoint Make You Stupid? *Presentations.* March 2004.

Skalak, David. Data Mining Blunders Exposed! *DB2 Magazine.* Quarter 2, 2001.

Snow, Colin. Keeping Score. *Data Management Review.* September 2006.

Songini, Marc L. Collections of Data. *Computerworld.* April 15, 2002.

Speak Up. *PM Network.* October 2006.

Spicer, Peter. Media Asset Overload. *Web Techniques.* December 1998.

Stein, Richard. Organizational Data Consumption: A Model for Comprehensive BPM Design. *Business Performance Management.* October 2004.

Strassmann, Paul A. Measuring Info Management. *Baseline Magazine.* May 2006.

Strassmann, Paul A. The Price of Dirty Data. *Baseline Magazine.* July 2006.

Strong, Diane M., Lee, Yang W., and Wang, Richard Y. Data Quality in Context. *Communications of the ACM.* May 1997.

Sullivan, Dan. 5 Principles of Intelligent Content Management. *Intelligent Enterprise.* August 31, 2001.

Surmacz, Jon. Searching for Answers. *CIO.* September 15, 2004.

Symons, George. Assessing the Value of Content: Information Management. *Data Management Review.* March 2004.

Tabaka, Jean. Too Many Time Zones. *Software Development Magazine.* January 2006.

Tayi, Giri T., and Ballou, Donald P. Examining Data Quality. *Communications of the ACM.* February 1998.

The Closeout. *Projects at Work.* May/June 2003.

Thomsen, Erik. Data vs. Knowledge. *Intelligent Enterprise.* April 10, 2000.

Thomsen, Erik. Information Impact: Business Analytics Renewed (Part 3). *Intelligent Enterprise.* August 31, 2001.

Thomsen, Erik. It's an Uncertain World. *Intelligent Enterprise.* December 1998.

Toigo, Jon W. Avoiding a Data Crunch. *Scientific American.* May 2000.

Too Much Information. *PM Network.* October 2006.

Top Reasons for Poor Project Performance. *PM Network.* May 2006.

Top 10 Project Management Challenges. *PM Network.* April 2004.

Tristram, Claire. Data Extinction. *Technology Review.* October 2002.

Typanski, Robert E. Creating an Effective Information Environment. *Information Systems Management.* Spring 1999.

Udell, Jon. Managing Metadata. *Infoworld.* October 24, 2005.

Vaughan, Jack. Taming the Torrent of Data. *Application Development Trends.* November 1999.

Veth, George. Scorecards: Translating Strategy into Action. *Data Management Review.* June 2006.

Wang, Richard Y. Total Data Quality Management. *Communications of the ACM.* February 1998.

Waters, John K. Reining in Unstructured Data. *Application Development Trends.* February 2005.

Wealth of Information. *PM Network.* July 2006.

Weglarz, Geoffrey. Two Worlds of Data: Structured and Unstructured. *Data Management Review.* September 2004.

Weldon, Jay-Louise and Joch, Alan. Data Warehouse Building Blocks. *Byte.* January 1997.

Westcott, Tom R. Sifting through Project Data: The Most Important Data Elements of Project Management. *Data Management Review.* June 2006.

Wheatley, Malcolm. Insight Unseen. *PM Network.* September 2006.

White, Colin. Data Integration: Still a Barrier for Most Organizations. *Data Management Review.* April 2006.

Whiting, Rick. Away Rubbish. *Informationweek.* May 8, 2006.

Whiting, Rick. Trend Spotters. *Informationweek.* September 5, 2005.

Winkler, Connie. Get the Picture. *Computerworld.* January 9, 2006.

Winter, Richard. Think Systematically. *Intelligent Enterprise.* March 1, 2000.

Wu, Jonathan. Creating a Structure for Governing Data. *Data Management Review.* September 2006.

Yoon, Younghoc. Discovering Knowledge in Corporate Data Bases. *Information Systems Management.* Spring 1999.

You've Got Mail, *PM Network.* May 2006.

Zachman, J. A. A Framework for Information Systems Architecture. *IBM Systems Journal.* Vol. 26, No. 3, 1987.

Zikopoulos, Paul C. Information at Your Service. *DB2 Magazine.* Quarter 1, 2006.

Glossary

Accessibility: Allowing people to access data and information according to specific rules.

Active listening: A listener attempts to understand as clearly as possible what the speaker said.

Active voice: A style of writing where the object of action is the subject of the sentence.

Administrative: Pertaining to topics like the security and ownership of data and information.

Administrators: A behavioral style that is task-oriented and low key, according to the Birkman Model.

Agenda: An outline of topics to address at a meeting, detailing length of time and responsibility.

Analysis: The decomposition of content into manageable components.

Analyzers: Individuals who are logical and analytical, according to the Herrmann Brain Dominance Model.

Attention deficit: Stakeholders paying less attention towards output from a repository due to lack of reliability in the content.

Birkman Model: A psychological typology that identifies behavioral styles that reflects one's perceptions and assumptions.

Black Hat thinking: A pattern of thinking that looks at the negative side when addressing problems, uses, and concerns.

Blue Hat thinking: A pattern of thinking that emphasizes organization and control when addressing problems, uses, and concerns.

Blue personalities: Individuals who are motivated by intimacy, reflection, and empathy, according to Taylor Hartman's Color Code guide to assessing personality traits.

Bodily-kinesthetic intelligence: A cognitive process that is exercised through physical action, according to the Multiple Intelligences Model.

Bosses: Individuals who are protective and take charge, according to the Enneagram.

Brain dominance: The side of the brain that dominates a person's thoughts and actions.

Cartwheel network: A variant of the circle network, whereby one node functions as a traffic cop with responsibility for regulating the quantity and quality of transmissions.

Checklists: A document that ensures that readers complete specific tasks.

Chronology format: The organization of content that stresses time sequence.

Circle network: A number of nodes connected, whereby each node relays a transmission sequentially to another.

Color Code: A psychological model that reflects traits as well as strengths and weaknesses of people in how they think, feel, and act.

Communications management plan: A document detailing the communications processes, tools, and techniques used on a project.

Communications process: An integrated and interdependent set of processes that enable exchange of data and information between two or more people.

Communicators: A behavioral style that is people-oriented and assertive, according to the Birkman Model.

Comparison and contrast format: The organization of content that presents differences and similarities between two topics.

Complainers: A category of difficult people who continually gripe but never offer a solution.

Complexity level: A mathematical formula to determine the number of communications channels used on a project.

Concurrent review: An approach for reviewing documentation that requires sending out multiple copies to reviewers.

Conditional (issues, facts, and conclusions format): The organization of content that employs an if/then construct.

Context: The setting or environment consisting of time, space, and structure that influences the quality and quantity of data and information transmitted.

Critical data: Content considered essential for the successful completion of a project.

Critical issues/action items log: A document used to capture and track concerns and tasks of importance to a project.

Database management system: Software that enables the access, storage, manipulation, and reporting of data residing in a system.

Data bias: Contents of a repository are skewed to satisfy a particular preference.

Data categories: Different classifications of data.

Data cleansing: Extracting the necessary data in a way that ensures the impurities of the content in the repository do not propagate into any information.

Data consumer: A stakeholder who uses the data in the repository.

Data custodian: A stakeholder who manages a repository and the supporting infrastructure.

Data incompleteness: Contents of a repository are lacking completeness, rendering the information useless.

Data inconsistency: Contents of a repository not stored in a consistent format.

Data incorrectness: Contents of a repository that are wrong which can result in bad information.

Data irrelevancy: Contents of a repository which are not germane to any of the activities of a project.

Data mart: A focused repository of data extracted from multiple data bases to meet a specific functional requirement.

Data mining: Stakeholders using their knowledge of the content, relationships, and patterns of the data within the repository to generate information.

Data presentation: The format and interpretation of data.

Data producer: A stakeholder who creates data to eventually populate the repository.

Data redundancy: Replication of content in a repository.

Data replication: The repository is populated from other systems at the right point in time to obtain relevancy of content and no loss of credibility.

Data reporting: Stakeholders employing a medium to communicate information to other stakeholders.

Data representation: The content and structure of the data and information residing in a repository.

Data smog: Lack of qualitative data that obscures efforts to generate clear, reliable information.

Data values: Issues that pertain to accuracy and consistency.

Data views: The model or models that exist to capture data.

Data visualization: Stakeholders extract information from the repository and put it in a comprehensible format.

Data warehouse: A system that allows the access, retrieval, and manipulation of data pulled from a repository of an operational system.

Data: Facts alone that are meaningless.

Decode: Deciphering messages to improve comprehension.

Defects: Faulty content within a repository.

Definitions format: The organization of content in the form of a glossary.

Devil's Advocates: Individuals who identify with the underdog and clash with authority, according to the Enneagram.

Effective listening: A listener attempts to understand the perspective of the speaker and exhibits empathy.

Encode: Crafting messages in a manner that allows the recipient to improve comprehension.

Enneagram: A psychological model that identifies nine personality types by patterns of behavior via unique thoughts and feelings.

Environment: The time, space, and structure of a context.

Epicures: Individuals who are dilettantes, according to the Enneagram.

Ethos: The moral or ethical content of a presentation.

Expediters: A behavioral style that is task-oriented and assertive, according to the Birkman Model.

Explanatory presentations: Talking before an audience with the goal of providing an understanding about how something works.

Extrovert: Individuals obtaining their energy from outside themselves according to the Myers–Briggs Temperament.

Feedback: The positive, negative, or neutral response from the sender.

Feeling: Individuals who are subjective by valuing intimacy over distance, according to the Myers–Briggs Temperament.

Flowcharts: A graphical display that depicts the flow of data, control, or strategy.

Forms: A medium for collecting data and information.

Garbage in, garbage out (GIGO): Bad data in a repository that results in incorrect information.

Givers: Individuals who are pursuers of approval and the affection of others, according to the Enneagram.

Glossary: A list of definitions for significant terms used on a project.

Green Hat thinking: A pattern of thinking that looks at different alternatives when addressing problems, uses, and concerns.

Group review: An approach for reviewing documentation that requires interactive participants from everyone at the same time.

Herrmann Brain Dominance: A typology used to understand human behavior using a quadrant-based model of the human brain.

Hierarchical network: A top-down or bottom-up arrangement of nodes that reflects the relative importance of each node in a communications network and allows for a message to travel multiple paths.

Hierarchy chart: A diagram showing the importance and relationship of the screens populating a Web site.

Hostile-aggressives: A category of difficult people who are pushy and use intimidation to have their way.

Hypothetical analyzers: Individuals who develop and weigh options before acting, according to Organizational Engineering.

Indecisives: A category of difficult people who cannot make decision or delay making one until forced to do so.

Information consumer: A stakeholder who uses information from a repository.

Information manufacturer: A stakeholder who provides sufficient support for a repository.

Information overload: Voluminous production of data and information to the point that the amount becomes incomprehensible.

Information supplier: A stakeholder who compiles information generated from a repository.

Information: Data processed in a manner that has meaning to the recipient.

Informative presentations: Talking before an audience with the goal of sharing information.

Integration: The relationship of each component of a PMIS in converting data into information.

Interdependence: The performance of one component influencing that of another one.

Interpersonal intelligence: A cognitive process that is exercised through dealing with other people, according to the Multiple Intelligences Model.

Intrapersonal intelligence: A cognitive process that is exercised through self-understanding, according to the Multiple Intelligences Model.

Introvert: Individuals obtaining their energy from an internal process, according to the Myers–Briggs temperament.

Intuitive: Individuals who look towards the future based upon their hunches and possibilities, according to the Myers–Briggs temperament.

Issues management: A process for identifying, capturing, and tracking critical important concerns and actions that exist.

Issues, facts, and conclusions format: The organization of content that describes a series of issues with each one followed by supporting facts.

Item-by-item procedure: A document that describes any topic, either sequentially or nonsequentially.

Judging: Individuals who emphasize finality, according to the Myers–Briggs temperament.

Know-it-alls: A category of difficult people who strive to impress and behave in a condescending manner.

Left brain dominance: The side of the brain which emphasizes facts, logical thinking, and reasoning.

Linear network: A sequential arrangement of nodes, whereby each node relays a message to a peer.

Linguistic intelligence: A cognitive process that is exercised through words, according to the Multiple Intelligences Model.

Logical Model: Displaying the needed functionalities to manage a project using a repository by describing what has to be done and not how and provides the basis for building the physical model.

Logical processors: Individuals who are logical and methodical, according to Organizational Engineering.

Logical–mathematical intelligence: A cognitive process that is exercised through logic, according to the Multiple Intelligences Model.

Logos: The logical content of a presentation.

Matrix: A document that compactly displays data and information under different conditions.

Mediators: Individuals who seek agreement, according to the Enneagram.

Medium: The tool used to transmit data and information between sender and receiver.

Meeting: An assembly of people with a specific purpose.

Message: Whether in hard or soft form, the content transmitted between the sender and receiver.

Meta data: Rules about data.

Methodology: The business rules for storing, accessing, and using a data repository under specific conditions.

Metrics: Measures employed to track cost, schedule, and quality performance on a project.

Middleware: Software that transparently links different applications.

Multiple Intelligences: A conceptual model that consists of unique cognitive processes which determine how one learns and responds to circumstances.

Musical Intelligence: A cognitive process that is exercised through sounds, according to the Multiple Intelligences Model.

Myers–Briggs Temperament: A psychological model predicated upon four categories of preferences.

Narrative procedure: A document which ensures that readers complete specific tasks.

Negativists: A category of difficult people who are fatalists.

Observers: Individuals who want their space, according to the Enneagram.

Organizational Engineering: A sociological model emphasizing complementary skills and compatibility among team members.

Organizers: Individuals who prefer structure and organization, according to the Herrmann Brain Dominance Model.

Paradigm: A model for perceiving and interpreting how the world works.

Passive voice: A style of writing whereby the recipient of action is the subject of the sentence.

Pathos: The emotional content of a presentation.

Perceiving: Individuals who emphasize options before making decisions, according to the Myers–Briggs Temperament.

Perfectionists: Individuals who have a prescriptive and normative focus, according to the Enneagram.

Performers: Individuals who are competitive and achievers, according to the Enneagram.

Personalizers: Individuals who like to interact with people and are expressive, according to the Herrmann Brain Dominance Model.

Persuasive presentations: Talking before an audience with the goal of convincing the members to think the same way or share an opinion.

Physical model: Displaying how all the hardware, people, software, and data interact with one another to realize the logical model.

Planners: A behavioral style that is people-oriented and low key, according to the Birkman Model.

Policy: One or more documents that provide broad guidelines on major topics.

Portability: The ability of an application to run on different platforms (e.g., operating systems).

Problem–Solution format: The organization of content that describes one or more problems and then provides one or more solutions.

Procedure: A document that covers the administrative and technical aspects of managing a project.

Process description format: The organization of content that takes the format of input, process, and output.

Process model: A description usually in graphic form, showing the components of a system (e.g., computing, manual, or combination) and how they interact with one another.

Product manager: A stakeholder who oversees the overall process of capturing and storing data as well as producing and distributing information.

Project management information system (PMIS): A repository consisting of hardware and software as well as data and information relevant to a project.

Project manual: An organized assembly of relevant project documentation in a binder or repository.

Reactive stimulators: Individuals who act right away, according to Organizational Engineering.

Readability index: A method for determining clarity and conciseness of documentation, such as the Fog Index and the Flesch–Kincaid Indices.

Receiver: The person who receives and decodes data and information from the sender.

Red Hat thinking: A pattern of thinking that uses emotion when addressing problems, uses, and concerns.

Red personalities: Individuals who are motivated by acquiring power, according to the Color Code.

Relational innovators: Individuals who define and redefine goals, according to Organizational Engineering.

Relational network: A patchwork of nodes with each one having a series of links, akin to a neural network.

Reports: A medium for disbursing data and information on the status of a project.

Repository: A pool of data and information about a project.

Right brain dominance: The side of the brain which emphasizes emotions and sensory perception.

Rush to judgment: Jumping to conclusions after taking only a cursory look at the data and information from repository.

Scalability: The ability of an application to accommodate growth without significant degradation in performance.

Sender: The person who transmits and encodes to one or more receivers.

Sensate: Individuals who are experiential based, according to the Myers–Briggs Temperament.

Serial Review: An approach for reviewing documentation that requires each reader to review a document one person at a time.

Silent and Nonresponsives: A category of difficult people who are reluctant to share feelings and thoughts.

Single point of contact (SPOC): The person designated to have responsibility to collect data and information to populate the content of a repository according to rules and standards.

Spatial arrangement format: The organization of content using location or geography.

Spatial intelligence: A cognitive process that is exercised through images, according to the Multiple Intelligences Model.

Stakeholder or customer format: The organization of content into groups according to relevance to people or organizations.

Stakeholders: The individuals or organizations who have a direct or indirect interest in a project.

Step-by-step procedure: A document that describes sequential or linear activities involving more than one person.

Sunset approach: The purging or archiving of contents of a repository to improve its usefulness.

Super-agreeables: A category of difficult people who never commit or produce anything that will result in controversy.

Synthesis: Assembling components of content into a meaningful composition to improve comprehension.

Systemic view: A description of the integration and interdependence of all the components and relationships of an entity.

Technology: The tools (e.g., hardware and software) used to support a project management information system.

Thinking Hats: A set of thinking patterns to address problems, issues, and concerns.

Thinking: Individuals who rely more on logic based upon the use of formal criteria and principles, according to the Myers–Briggs Temperament.

Topical format: The organization of content that covers subjects according to some order.

Tragic Romantics: Individuals who are idealistic, according to the Enneagram.

Virtual meetings: The electronic assembly of people to address a specific purpose.

Visualizers: Individuals who are visionaries and see the overall picture, according to the Herrmann Brain Dominance Model.

War room: A facility that provides stakeholders with a location to communicate and collaborate.

Web site: A medium for displaying project information using Internet technology.

White Hat thinking: A pattern of thinking that emphasizes facts, data, objectivity, and independence when addressing problems, uses, and concerns.

White personalities: Individuals who are motivated through peace, according to the Color Code.

Yellow Hat thinking: A pattern of thinking that emphasizes benefits and taking a constructive approach when addressing problems, uses, and concerns.

Yellow personalities: Individuals who are motivated by excitement, according to the Color Code.

Index

A

Abstract thinkers, 58
Active listening, *see* Listening, active and
    effective
Administrative monolith, 36
Administrators, 49
Analyzers, 56, 57
Arc of distortion, message, 14
Attention deficit, 31
Audit
    process-oriented, 33
    trail, documentation and, 84
Automated scheduling tools, 12

B

Behavioral science, 46
Behavior patterns
    CMP norms and, 74
    models identifying, 45
Big picture people, 57
Birkman model, 49
Black Hat thinking, 117, 118
Blue Hat thinking, 117, 118
Blue personalities, 50
Bodily-kinesthetic intelligence, 52
Body language
    best approach for interpreting, 15
    confident, 143
    message receptivity and, 138
Bosses, motivator of, 55

Brain, quadrant-based model of, 56
Broadcasting media, 12

C

Center for Business Practice, management
    challenges identified by, 2
Central processor units (CPUs), 172
Chain of logic, 132
Change board meeting, agenda for, 114
Charts, use of in documentation, 97
Checklists, purpose of, 101
Checkpoint review, agenda for, 112
Circle network, 18
CMP, *see* Communications management plan,
    issues management process and
Color code summary table, 50
Color model, 50
Common Oriented Request Broker
    Architecture (CORBA), 30
Communications
    definition of, 5
    diagram, 9
    failure, 3, 73
    infrastructure, 13
    process, 5, 6
        ambiguity of, 14
        feedback, 8
        medium, 7
        message quality, 8
        relevant factors, 7
        setting of, 8

variables surrounding, 15
rigidity in, 7
skill, hardest, 68
subjectivity of, 6, 7
truths, 3
Communications management plan (CMP),
  issues management process and,
  71–82
  communications management plan, 72
    challenges, 73–74
    characteristics, 72–73
    development, deployment, and
      maintenance of, 75–78
    drafting of, 77
    flowchart, 75
    implementation suggestions, 78
    meat of, 76
    promotion of, 77
    purposes of, 72
    structure of, 75
  getting started checklist, 81–82
  issues management process, 79
    challenges, 80
    flowchart, 79
    governance process, 79
  PMIS contributions, 71–72
  significant contributor, 80
Communicators, 49
Complainers, 119
Control room, view of as asset, 181
CORBA, *see* Common Oriented Request
  Broker Architecture
Corporate culture, meetings and, 110
Cost performance index (CPI), 32, 53
Costs, higher, bad communications and, 3
CPI, *see* Cost performance index
CPUs, *see* Central processor units
Critical issues/action item log, 80
Customer
  communication with, 1
  environment, project managers dealing
    with, 126

D

Daily standup meeting, agenda for, 114
Data
  bad, 33
  bias, 33

cleansing, 34
consumers, stakeholders as, 28
duplicate, 32
dynamic capture of, 31
ecological perspective of, 40
environmental conditions, 31
flood of, 5
flow
  diagram (DFD), 101
  process model of, 34
garbage bin of, 31, 170
hoarding, 36
inconsistency, 32
irrelevant, 32
linkages among, 39
management, incorrect thinking about,
    185–186
mart, 34
mining, 34
proprietary, 35–36
purge, 33
quality, 33
query tools, 35
redundant, 32, 39
replication, 35
sharing, 35
silos, 39
smog, 31
stakeholder treatment of, 36
tainted, 32, 38
views, 33–34
warehouse, 34
Web site, 170
Database management system (DBMS), 26
DBMS, *see* Database management system
DCE, *see* Distributed Computing Environment
Deep dives, presentation during, 126
Devil's advocates, 54, 55
DFD, *see* Data flow diagram
Diagrams, use of in documentation, 97
Difficult people summary table, 119
Distributed Computing Environment (DCE),
    30
Documentation
  approach to determining readability of, 85
  bias, 91
  changes, 97
  choice of language, 90
  configuration control of, 96
  copyright law and, 103
  creation, 90

detail, 92
example of project procedure, 98
feedback, 91, 95
flowchart, 87
goals of, 88
grammatical rules for, 94
group review of, 95
importance of, 84
inadequate, 104
layout, 94
manuscript revision, 96
most common, 102
parts of, 91
relevancy, 93
translation of, 85
use of parallel structure in, 94
versatility in creating, 85
Documentation, drafting and publishing of,
       83–107
   documentation phases, 86–97
      approval or disapproval, 96
      distribution, 96–97
      draft, 86–95
      maintaining and updating documents,
         97
      manuscript revision, 96
      review, 95–96
   documentation types, 98–102
   getting started checklist, 104–107
   PMIS contributions, 83
   project manager as writer, 85–86
   project manual, 103–104
   right amount, 104
   supporting material, 97–98
   too little importance, 84
   why writing matters, 83–84
Do gooders, 50

E

Effective listening, *see* Listening, active and
         effective
E-mail
   announcement of Web site, 172
   chain, 13
   communication by, 74
   feedback via, 79
   flame, 17
   flood of data with, 36

Emotional baggage, word choice having, 16
Enneagram, 53
Epicures, 54, 55
Ethos, example of, 132
Executives, communication with, 1
Expediters, 49, 50
Explanatory presentations, 127, 129
Extroverts, introverts versus, 47
Eye contact, importance of, 16

F

Facts and data, 134, 143
Fax, communication by, 74
Feedback
   assumptions, 17
   best approach for handling, 14
   CMP, 77
   connotative interpretation, 15
   document, 91, 95
   IMP, 79
   incongruent behaviors in, 16
   types of, 8, 13
   variables influencing, 17
Feeling people, thinking people versus, 47
Flesch–Kincaid Indices, 85
Flowchart(s)
   challenge of, 101
   meetings, 111
   presentation, 129
   types of, 101
   war room, 176
   Web site, 169
Fog Index, 85
Forms, 99
Functional managers, communication with, 1
Fun lovers, 51

G

Garbage in, garbage out (GIGO), 32
GIGO, *see* Garbage in, garbage out
Givers, 54, 55
Glossary, 102, 199–207
Governance process, IMP, 79
Green Hat thinking, 117, 118
Gresham's Law of Data, 33

H

HA, *see* Hypothetical Analyzer
Halo effect, message interpretation and, 67
Hearing
    actions of, 65
    selective, 66, 67
Herrmann Brain Dominance typology, 56
Hierarchical network, 19, 20
Hierarchy chart, 171
Hostile-Aggressives, 119
Hypothetical Analyzer (HA), 57, 58, 59

I

IMP, *see* Issues management process
Indecisives, 120
Information
    consumers, 28
    misconstrued, 10
    overload, 31
    power of, 187
    unreliable, 186
InformationWeek, 2
Informative presentations, 127, 128
Intellectual capital, 103
Intelligence, types of, 51–52
Internet, research material found on, 86
Interpersonal intelligence, 52
Interpersonal skills, documentation and, 85
Interviews, documentation preparation using, 88
Intrapersonal intelligence, 52
Introverts, extroverts versus, 47
Intuitive people, sensates versus, 47
Issues management process (IMP), 71, *see also*
        Communications management plan,
        issues management process and
IT leadership failure, 2

J

Judging people, perceiving people versus, 47

K

Kinesics, 15
Know-It-Alls, 120
Knowledge transfer, documentation and, 84

L

Leadership, effective, 185–187
    disciplines, 186
    leadership, 186–187
    PMIS requirement of good data, 185–186
Linear network, 18, 19
Linguistic intelligence, 51, 52
Listening
    difficulty of, 64
    flowchart, 65
    skills, document preparation and, 89
Listening, active and effective, 63–70
    active and effective listening, 63–64
    getting started checklist, 68–70
    important reasons, 64
    most important skill, 68
    PMIS contributions, 63
    steps, 65–68
        clarify, 66–67
        hear, 65–66
        interpret, 67
        respond, 67–68
    why few people listen effectively, 64–65
Logical designs, concentration of, 30
Logical–mathematical intelligence, 52
Logical model, 36, 37
Logical Processor (LP), 57, 58, 59
Logos, presentation, 132
LP, *see* Logical Processor

M

Matrices, information displayed in, 101
Media
    broadcasting, 12
    choice of, 11–12
    informal, 13
Mediators, communication style of, 55
Meeting(s), 109–124
    agenda for, 112

avoidance of, 121
bad eggs, 119–120
categories of, 126
change board, 114
civility guidelines, 121
conducting, 113–115
counterproductive, 109
daily standup, 114
flowchart, 111
follow-up on results, 115
getting started checklist, 122–124
guidelines, 115
impasse, 116–118
indicators of poor meetings, 110–111
kickoff, attention getter in, 133–134
planning, 111–113
PMIS contributions, 109
reasons for meeting failure, 110
reasons for meetings, 109–110
rules, 121
stalemates, 117
status review, 113
steps for successful meetings, 111
virtual meetings, 115–116
worst and best of times, 121
Memo, well written, 91
Mental models, meeting impasse and, 116
Message(s)
arc of distortion in, 14
categories of, 10
forms of, 7
interpretation, halo effect and, 67
medium used to communicate, 7
misperceived, 9
noise affecting, 14
quality of, 8
receptivity, body language and, 138
tailoring of to appropriate audience, 4
urgency of sending, 11
Metadata rules, establishment of, 32
Microsoft Outlook, 181
Model(s)
behavior patterns, 45
Birkman, 49
color, 50
logical, 36, 37
mental, meeting impasse and, 116
Myers–Briggs temperament types, 46
physical, PMIS, 36, 38
Multicultural project, 85
Multiple intelligences, 51, 52

Musical intelligence, 52
Myers–Briggs temperament, 46–48

N

Negativists, 120
Network
circle, 18
hierarchical, 19, 20
linear, 18, 19
relational, 19, 20, 21
wheel, 18, 19
Y, 18, 20
Noise, 8
Nonexistent dialogue, 74

O

Observers, 54, 55
OE, *see* Organizational engineering
Organizational engineering (OE), 9, 57, 58
Organizers, 56, 57

P

Paradigm shifts, 117
Pathos, project management example of, 132
Peace keepers, 51
Perceiving people, judging people versus, 47
Perfectionists, 54, 55
Performers, 54
Personality(ies)
Blue, 50
Red, 50
style, 45–61
Birkman model, 49–50
caveats, 45–46
color code, 50–51
Enneagram, 53–56
getting started checklist, 60–61
Herrmann Brain Dominance, 56–57
many models, 59
multiple intelligences, 51–53
Myers–Briggs temperament, 46–48
organizational engineering, 57–59
types, relationships between, 53

White, 51
Yellow, 51
Personalizers, 56, 57
Persuasive presentations, 127, 129
Physical model, PMIS, 36, 38
Pinging, 14
Planners, 49
PMBOK, *see* Project Management Body of
    Knowledge
PMI, *see* Project Management Institute
PMIS, *see* Project Management Information
    System
PMS, *see* Project management system
Policy, example of, 98
Power wielders, 50
Presentation(s), 125–165
    attention getters in, 144
    characteristics of effective presentation,
        127–129
    credibility of, 143
    cultural considerations, 140
    delivery, 140–151, 152
    distracting mannerisms, 140
    emotional content of, 132
    enumeration in, 134
    explanatory, 127, 129
    eye contact in, 148
    flip charts used in, 151
    flowchart, 129
    getting started checklist, 153–165
    handouts in, 150
    humor in, 148
    ineffective, 126
    informative, 127, 128
    loss of effectiveness, 126–127
    opportunities to present, 125–126
    overhead projector use in, 150
    persuasive, 127, 129
    PMIS contributions, 125
    post delivery, 151–152
    preparation, 130–137, 152
    proportionality of, 132
    rehearsal, 137–139, 152
    room configuration, 142
    semantics, 140
    site survey, 138
    stage fright, 143–144
    strategy, 131
    tactics, 131
    timing, 141
    types, 127

    videotaping of, 139
    view foils and slides in, 150
    virtual tools, 11
    visual aids used in, 135
    visualization of, 139
    ways to keep audience attention, 146, 147
    ways to wake up audience, 147
Procedure(s)
    example of, 98, 100, 101
    types of, 98
Project
    background information, 131
    competence, 1
    failure, likelihood of, 25
    life cycle, communications throughout, 4
    manual, 103–104
    multicultural, 85
    procedure, example of, 98, 100, 101
    self-analysis, 130
    staff meeting, agenda for, 112
    status review meetings, 79
Project communications management, elements
        of, 1–24
    communications process, 5–7, 7–8
    communications truths, 3–5
    difficulty of process, 22
    feedback, 13–15
    getting started checklist, 23–24
    medium, 11–13
    message, 10–11
    principal vehicle, 21–22
    sender and receiver, 8–10
    setting, 17–20
    variables, 15–17
Project Management Body of Knowledge
        (PMBOK), 40
Project Management Information System
        (PMIS), 2, 45
    accessibility, 35
    activities, 27
    anachronistic, 31
    automated, 28
    behavior pattern, 27
    consequences of, 31
    contributions
        CMP, 71–72
        documentation, 83
        IMP, 71–72
        listening, 63
        meetings, 109
        presentations, 125

war rooms, 175
Web site development, 167
data representation, 30
definition of, 25
establishment of, 25–43
    data versus information, 30–34
    definition and components, 25–26
    development of automated PMIS,
        28–30
    fine distinction, 40
    getting started checklist, 41–43
    key characteristics, 27
    keys to meaningful PMIS, 35–40
    never-ending construction, 40
    repository types, 34–35
    roles, 28
flowchart, 29
forms and reports, 26
as garbage bin of data, 31
as instrument of power, 186
integration, 27
interdependence, 27
key functions of, 21–22
leadership and, 185
listening and, 63
logical model, 36, 37
meeting management using, 109
methodology, 26
output quality of, 37
performance statistics, 38
physical model, 36, 38
policies, 26
portability, 30
project communications management skills
        and, 21
repository, 25
scalability, 30
self-audit of, 33, 34
supporting infrastructure for, 37
technology, 26
Project Management Institute (PMI), 40
Project management system (PMS), 40
Project managers
    communications truths facing, 3
    documentation research by, 88
    failure to ask questions, 67
    interaction of with people in organization,
        125
    as linchpins, 2, 22, 64, 125
    meetings initiated by, 110

    need for flexibility when
        communicating, 5
    as writers, 85

Q

Query results, 35

R

RAM, *see* Random access memory
Random access memory (RAM), 172
RDMS, *see* Relational database management
        system
Reactive Stimulator (RS), 57, 58
Red Hat thinking, 117
Red personalities, 50
Relational database management system
        (RDMS), 28
Relational Innovator (RI), 57, 58, 59
Relational network, 19, 20, 21
Reports, 102
Repository(ies)
    data, sunset approach, 38
    rules for populating, 39
    types of, 34
    updates, timing of, 35
RI, *see* Relational Innovator
Right-brain thinking, examples of, 65
RS, *see* Reactive Stimulator

S

Sarbanes-Oxley Act, 75
Satellites, communication by, 74
Schedule performance index (SPI), 32,
        53, 118
Selective attention, 15
Selective hearing, 66, 67
Self-audit, PMIS, 33, 34
Semantics, 15, 16
Senior managers, communication with, 1
Sensates, intuitive people versus, 47
Silent and Non-Responsives, 120
Single point of contact (SPOC), 39
Spatial intelligence, 51

SPI, *see* Schedule performance index
SPOC, *see* Single point of contact
SQL, *see* Structured query language
Stage fright, presentations and, 143–144
Stakeholder(s)
    backgrounds of, 64
    bad communications among, 2
    CMP-noncompliant, 78
    communications preferences of, 4
    communication style of, 45
    as data consumers, 28
    disagreements of, 6
    document reading by, 88
    executive-level, 4
    hat determination of, 118
    identification of, 71
    indecisive, 120
    interest of, 26
    issues presented by, 79
    know-it-all, 120
    meeting avoidance by, 121
    meeting involvement of, 113
    negative feedback received by, 15
    project manager communication with, 1
    repository use by, 21
    roles of, 28
    silent, 120
    super-agreeable, 120
    treatment of data by, 36
    trust among, 12
    Web site access by, 167
Statistics, use of in presentations, 133
Status review meeting, agenda for, 113
Structured query language (SQL), 28
Super-Agreeables, 120

T

Tables, use of in documentation, 97
Team identity, Web site and, 168
Teleconferencing, 11
Thinking hats summary table, 117
Thinking people, feeling people versus, 47
Thinking styles, 8–9
Tragic romantics, 54, 55

U

User site licenses, 28

V

Videoconferencing, 11, 12, 74
Virtual meetings, 115
Visual aids
    cardinal rule for, 136
    characteristics of, 136
    pitfalls to avoid, 149
    types of, 135
Visualizers, 57
Vital Smarts magazine, 1
Vocal variety, 16

W

War rooms, 175–183
    advantages, 175
    asset, 181
    building of, 177
    challenges, 180–181
    cleanliness of, 180
    customers invited to, 176
    display of information, 177
    flowchart, 176
    function of, 175
    getting started checklist, 182–183
    ill-equipped, 181
    maintenance, 177, 180
    PMIS contributions, 175
    purpose, 177
    steps, 176–180
    wall number 1, 178
    wall number 2, 179
    wall number 3, 179
Web-based technology, documentation
    development using, 86
Web conferencing, communication by, 74
Webex, 11, 76
Web site
    data types, 170
    design heuristics, 171
    development and deployment, 167–174
        advantages, 167–168

challenges, 168
getting started checklist, 173–174
guidelines, 168–172
PMIS contributions, 167
sharing and visibility, 173
documents stored on, 97
flowchart, 169
hierarchy chart, 171
stakeholder visits of, 172
team identity and, 168
update schedule, 172
Wheel network, 18, 19

White Hat thinking, 117, 118
White personalities, 51
Writers, project managers as, 85
Writing, importance of, 83, 84

Y

Yellow Hat thinking, 117, 118
Yellow personalities, 51
Y network, 18, 20